The Orvis Guide to
FLY FISHING FOR CARP

Tips and Tricks for the
Determined Angler

Kirk Deeter

STONEFLY
PRESS

PO Box 6146
Bloomington, IN 47407
FAX: 877-609-3814

For information about discounts on bulk purchases, or to
book the author for an engagement or demonstration, please
contact Stonefly Press at info@stoneflypress.com,
or visit us as StoneflyPress.com.

Printed in the United States of America

17 16 15 14 13 1 2 3 4 5

MIX
Paper from
responsible sources
FSC® C002589

Library of Congress Control Number: 2012955950

———————————————————————

Stonefly Press

Publisher: Robert D. Clouse

Acquiring Editor: David A. Gray

Managing Production Editor: Bill Bowers

Copy Editor: Bill Bowers

Proofreader: Eileen McNulty

Cover Designer: Al Quattrocchi

Front Cover Photo: Kevin Morlock

Back Cover Photo: Tim Romano

Photo on page i by Steve Martinez
Photos on pp. 17, 19, 24, 25, and 46 © 2013 by Shutterstock

*This book is dedicated to the late, great Charlie Meyers,
outdoors columnist for The Denver Post
and my writing mentor*

CONTENTS

ACKNOWLEDGMENTS

*T*his book wouldn't have been possible were it not for all the "brownliners" out there who want to change fly fishing for the better. I want to thank my wife, Sarah, and son, Paul, for their support as I fish and write about that. Thanks to my parents, and my brother and his family, for their encouragement to chase a dream. Thanks to Sallie Warner (the book for Fred is coming up next).

I appreciate the help and partnership of Tim Romano, one of the best photographers I know, but an even better person—and not just because he allowed me to lift some of his images for this book. Thanks also to Chris Hunt for an inspiring and eloquent foreword. Thank you Al Quattrocchi, for a great cover.

To Geoff Mueller, Tom Bie, Gregg Arnold, Greg Thomas, Anthony Licata, Dave Hurteau, Dietmar Grimm, Conway Bowman, Kevin Morlock, Steve Martinez, Kent Klewein, Louis Cahill, Chris Santella, J.P. Lipton, Jeff Currier, Will Rice, John Bartlett, Michael Gracie, John Hendrickson, Bruce Smithhammer, Dave Maynard, and of course, Barry Reynolds. I'm in your debt. Heartfelt thanks also to John Frasier, Erin Block, Jay Zimmerman, Tom Reed, Brian Schmidt, John Davenport, Paul Rose, Tim Daughton, Cameron Mortenson, Kyle Perkins, Clint Packo, Ryan Dunne, and David Moore. I'll see you all on the water.

ABOUT THE AUTHOR

*K*irk Deeter is the editor of *TROUT* magazine and an editor-at-large for *Field & Stream*. He is coeditor of *Field & Stream's* "Fly Talk" blog at fieldandstream .com, "Fly Fishing Jazz" columnist for MidCurrent.com, and editor-in-chief of *Angling Trade* magazine. Kirk is the author of five books, including *The Little Red Book of Fly Fishing* (coauthored with the late *Denver Post* outdoors editor Charlie Meyers).

Deeter has won numerous Excellence in Craft honors for magazine feature writing from the Outdoor Writers Association of America, and his essay "Carp Crazy" (illustrated by Ralph Steadman) was listed in *America's Best Sports Writing*. He is known for his offbeat story angles: chasing mako sharks from kayaks . . . teaching Eskimos to be fly-fishing guides . . . fishing for arapaima and tarpon in the jungles of Guyana . . . the fishing-golf connection in Ireland . . . and scuba diving (aka "Going Deep") with northern pike, bass, and trout. His work has also appeared in *The New York Times*, *Garden & Gun*, *The Drake*, *Fly Fisherman*, *Fly Rod & Reel*, *Big Sky Journal*, *SaltWater Sportsman*, London's *Daily Telegraph*, *The Denver Post*, and elsewhere. He lives near Denver, Colorado, with his wife, Sarah, and son, Paul.

Photo by Steve Martinez

Erin Block. *Photo by Jay Zimmerman*

FOREWORD

*I*zaak Walton, in his treatise *The Compleat Angler,* described carp as ". . . the queen of rivers, a stately, a good and very subtil fish." Perhaps it's fitting that Walton lived in England. Today, more than 350 years later, the Brits still think highly of carp, as do many anglers in continental Europe.

Here in the U.S., carp are mostly held in disdain. I think it has to do with their unsightly appearance when compared to other, more "worthy" gamefish. Their big, rubbery mouths don't do them many favors in the glamour division, and the barbels that grow from their upper lips mark them as lowly bottom feeders to the uninitiated.

And while many of us probably caught carp as kids, we've likely moved on to more "acceptable" targets, like trout and bass.

Do yourself a favor. Think back to your childhood. Chances are you were catching perhaps the world's perfect gamefish on dough balls and corn. I'm also guessing, if you were like me, you took twisted glee as carp slyly stole the crusts of bread you tossed to the ducks in some soupy city pond.

I think being a kid in the city was the perfect excuse to catch carp on purpose.

For me, carp might have been my first real childhood diversion—they were ready to play on the ideal summer days I'd spend sitting in the grass at Stern Lake in Littleton, Colorado, my head in the clouds and my line in the dark, questionable water. Girls were still gross, and my brothers were in diapers. Carp, though, were always home and seemingly always willing to stretch a fishing line tight.

The park was a 10-minute bike ride from home, and if it was too hot to be catching crawdads in the ditch across the street, I knew I could lie back on the cool grass beneath a giant weeping willow at Stern Lake and only be interrupted when the flour, salt, and water concoction that I'd cook up in my mother's kitchen had another taker.

And my mother was none too fond of my dalliances with carp. First, the fish lived in the pond alongside other less-than-desirable critters. She was convinced that all muskrats were rabid and that carp, by association, were, to say the least, unclean.

When I'd bring a bucket of live carp home and put them in a big steel washtub full of hose water in the backyard, she'd react poorly. Not as poorly as the time

I tipped a box full of garter snakes over in the living room, but poorly just the same.

Sadly, I outgrew carp, and I don't think it was voluntary—I think the stigma that came with fishing for carp eventually grew too much for an 8-year-old kid to handle. You can only hear from your parents or from the passersby at the park that carp are trash fish so many times. Eventually, you come to believe it.

I've always fished, and for the last 20 years or so, I've fly fished. But it took me decades to come back to carp, and not because I could lie back on the bank of a pond and dream away an afternoon while fishing for them. I came back to carp quite by accident.

About 10 years ago, I was following a tip from a friend of mine in Pocatello, Idaho, who told me the Snake River was a burgeoning smallmouth bass fishery. He etched some crude directions on some scrap paper to a place on the Snake where smallies were building redds and spawning beneath the sweeping high-desert skies of southern Idaho. Knowing I was a newspaper editor at the time, his only admonition to me was, "If you ever write about fishing for smallmouth there, I'll beat you bloody."

I drove the crop-lined roads along the Snake, heading downstream below American Falls Reservoir, noting that the landscape was quite barren. Sagebrush took over when sprouting spuds, barley, and sugar beets played out, and eventually the road turned to loose gravel and I was in the desert, miles away from town. I followed the directions carefully, and about an hour after I left home, I arrived at a little backwater slough on the Snake.

I strung up a 4-weight, thinking I'd get some real play out of foot-long smallies from the bank on the light rod, and wandered to the water. It was early May, and spring was coming to the desert. A lonely Russian olive was nearly all leafed out, and a sweetwater spring gurgled to the surface from a moraine of lava rock the lined the little bay.

I cast a small Bugger into the water and began a slow, methodical strip.
Nothing.

I kept at it for an hour or so with nothing to show for the effort. Eventually, I gave up.

Back at my truck, my back to the water, I began to break down my gear. I heard a raucous splash, and turned around in time to see a host of rings traveling along the water's surface away from a pool of bubbly water. I looked intently into the green, foggy water through polarized lenses, but I couldn't tell what had caused the ruckus.

I turned my back on the river again to continue disassembling my gear, and another massive splash shook the slough behind me. I whipped around quickly, but again, I could see only what was left behind. Frothy water.

Chris Hunt
Photo by Kirk Deeter

I looked over the otherwise quiet slough, and I even glanced into the evening sky, thinking that perhaps what was causing the splashes was falling from the heavens. My mind began to wander, and I couldn't help but wonder if perhaps parts of some disabled satellite were falling to Earth, or perhaps an overflying jet had managed to jettison a couple of Samsonites.

Then it happened again. There, not 30 feet from where I stood, a massive fish erupted from the water and fell back down again. I knew what it was the second I saw it—although I don't ever remember seeing a carp quite so big. I paused in the process of putting my gear away—I only had the little 4-weight with me, so I knew I had no hope of landing one of those massive fish. But hooking one . . . and playing one . . . that would be pretty damn fun.

I looked around. I was alone. Who would know?

I reconstructed my rod, shortened my leader, and dug through my fly box for something suitable for such a behemoth. All the while, the splashing continued.

Finally, I settled on a white, rabbit fur creation I'd tied for surf perch while living on the Northern California coast, and I ventured to the river. After a few poorly executed casts of the heavy fly on the light rod, I figured I either had to give up, or I had to go big. I had to get in the water. And it was gross water—my mother would have died if she saw me dip my toes into the green stew that the carp had churned up.

But to my surprise, it was only about shin-deep, and the bottom was mostly firm. I waded out onto what I now call "the flat," and began to chuck-and-duck with the big, heavy fly and supple little 4-weight. I watched as the carp frolicked all around me—there were dozens of them. It took about an hour, but my line finally stretched tight. Using what little big-water fly-fishing skill I possessed, I stripped hard, hoping to set the hook. All hell broke loose.

I remember the little prayer I said as I watched my backing knot slip through the tip-top of my rod. I remember seeing bare spool. And then I remember, for the first time in my life as a fisherman, giving chase. I trudged through shin-deep water until it was thigh-deep. Then it was waist-deep. Finally, I remember my T-shirt floating in a comical little skirt just under my armpits. Slowly—very slowly—I began to retrieve line. As the sun began to set in the west, and chill of the Idaho evening began to kick in, I knew I had to force the issue. I was shivering in chest-deep water, underequipped for such a battle, but also unwilling to really give up.

I began to pull back with everything the little 4-weight had, and I managed to back out of the water to where my waistline was dry. But with every turn of the spool I'd make, I'd eventually lose two.

Finally, and mercifully, the line went slack. I lost the fish.

Today, a decade later, carp are without a doubt my favorite freshwater fly-rod targets. They're stronger—much stronger—than trout. They make bass look like idiots. And they're more adaptable than any fish I know—they can live in the cold, clear waters of Bear Lake or the warm, polluted stew of the C&O Canal in the heart of Washington, D.C. They swim happily in the waters of the South Platte and the Henry's Fork, and they do just as well alongside alligators and cottonmouths in south Florida. No, they're not native. But they're also not going anywhere—they're so widely distributed throughout the U.S. that any effort to eradicate them would be folly.

So I fish for them. Happily.

I've also watched as the number of fly fishers interested in pursuing carp has grown—the carp is slowly acquiring a well-deserved following. And, in the following pages, I have no doubt that my friend Kirk Deeter—perhaps the most savvy fly fisher I know—will let you in on a few secrets to chasing carp on the fly. But, knowing Kirk, I'm sure he'll also leave quite a bit up to you. Exploring is something we anglers do very well, and with carp, there's a lot of exploring to do. First, though, I'd start right outside your front door—chances are, there are carp swimming somewhere within just a few miles of where you sit reading this book.

Enjoy the journey that comes with fly fishing for carp. And leave your 4-weight home.

—*Chris Hunt, National Communications Director, Trout Unlimited,*
and creator of the popular weblog eatmorebrooktrout.com

Introduction

Carp fishing with flies is a journey. Not so much a journey that can be measured in miles, but rather a journey that's measured in attitude.

We all start in different places for different reasons. For some, carp are the "because they're there" fish. Odds are, no matter where you are reading this, if the common carp isn't the fish swimming closest to you right now, it's not far away.

For others, carp are novelty fish. Trash fish. "Let's see if I can make that thing eat a fly . . ."

And yet, for millions around the globe, carp are actually "top of the game." Sacred fish. Most Americans simply cannot imagine the hours and money dedicated to catching carp worldwide. In many places, they're a bigger deal than trout, bass, pike, stripers, tarpon, and bonefish combined.

I once made the correlation in *Field & Stream* magazine between carp fishing and soccer—the rest of the world is stark, raving mad about both, but many Americans just don't get either. Maybe that's because we have splendid options to chase in our waters. My friend, the great outdoor writer and editor John Merwin, once told me bluntly: "If all the Europeans had the trout, pike, and bass we have in America, they'd give up the carp fascination."

I, for one, have tried to be a soccer fan, but I'm not giving up my passion for baseball, American football, or hockey anytime soon. And likewise, there's something special about a native cutthroat trout rising to a dry fly in a mountain stream. Jump one tarpon with a fly rod and your whole world will be rocked forever.

But even if the carp journey starts with, "because they're there," it soon evolves to "because I can." And not long after that, for some fly fishermen (and women), it goes to "because it makes me a better angler."

1

Charlie Meyers and Kirk Deeter. *Photo by Will Rice*

You see, the thing is, carp are no suckers—not literally nor figuratively. They're wary. They're cunning. They're the ultimate piscine "survivalists." They live in warm water, cold water, moving water, still water, dirty water, clean water . . . and they fight. They're hard enough to catch on conventional tackle (a whole other ball of wax . . . or corn . . . or "boilies" . . . or "glugged" bait piles launched via "spod"), but if you can figure out how to do so on the fly, you're onto something special.

You'd be surprised how many of the fly-fishing personalities you see on television or read in books and magazines are nuts about carp fishing in their "time off." Why? Because no matter where you find them, carp are fickle, and they aren't easy to fool—especially not with flies. They spook easily. They have the ability to signal danger to other carp around them. They're omnivores, so you can't rely on any given fly pattern on any given day. The rules constantly change. Fly fishing for carp is the ultimate test of innovation and trickery.

If you learn to fly fish for carp and do that well, you will inevitably develop skills that can be transposed to any trout river, or any saltwater flat, in America and beyond.

Now, I'm not naïve enough to think I'm going to convince everyone to love carp. You either get it or you don't. The "why" of carp fishing boils down to two things: because carp are virtually everywhere, and because carp can make you a good fly angler.

This is a "how" book designed to help anglers who already get at least one of the two reasons "why." I think the more trial, error, and ultimately, success you experience with carp, the more apt you'll be to consider them "golden gods" rather than "trash fish." In other words, all the pieces come together, and the rest takes care of itself.

As such, I hope the lessons to follow will start you on a journey that changes your perception of fly fishing. It's worth it. Trust me.

—*Kirk Deeter*
Pine, Colorado

Photo at right by Kevin Morlock

PART ONE · WORTHY QUARRY

Photo by Tim Romano

Why Carp?

*W*hen I told my mother I was writing a book on fly fishing for carp, her first response was, "Why would you do that?" She related a childhood story of how she hooked a carp while fishing with her father below the Independence Dam in Defiance, Ohio, and he laughed and laughed as that big, ugly fish tugged her up and down the riverbank. Back then—and to this day—the carp is considered by many anglers to be an unfortunate result. It's the fish you hook by accident. Most people certainly wouldn't think of eating carp (at least not these days). And to target carp intentionally with a fly rod, rather than a bow and arrow . . . well, that's just nuts.

Unless you really like to fly fish. And unless you really want to get good at fly fishing.

There is no doubt that the fly-fishing world spins on the axis of trout. Most of us start with trout. Most of the companies that make and sell things like rods, reels, lines, and other gear would not exist were it not for trout.

Saltwater fly fishing is almost an entirely different sport than fly fishing for trout. Same basic tools, totally different approach. On a trout stream, presentation is paramount. How that fly behaves after it hits the water is as important as, or more important than, the cast you make to get it there in the first place. In the salt, on the other hand, a great cast (long and accurate) is usually the price of admission.

We can debate the importance of other factors like the angler's ability to read water, and fly pattern selection, and the other intangibles that go into various types of fly fishing until we're blue in our faces. I've heard those conversations over and over. And my short answer is that all of it is important. No angler has ever suffered by having a great, accurate cast. You might not need to throw a fly 80 feet all the time, especially not on a trout stream, but it's pretty nice to have that distance in your arsenal. You don't need to be an entomologist or a marine biologist to decide on the right fly, but the more you understand what fish actually eat, the more fish you catch. And it never hurts to be able to spot fish and understand the subtle telltales that indicate where they will be at any given time.

Which is what brings me back to carp. Carp do a better job of demanding all the skills an angler can muster—from the accurate cast, to spotting fish, to picking the right bug, to dropping that fly right into the feeding zone at exactly the right moment and making it behave just so—than almost any fish you can chase with a fly rod.

Carp are tough, dogged fighters.
Photo by Kevin Morlock

A carp in the Los Angeles River. *Photo by Al Quattrocchi*

Carp Are Difficult to Pattern

*S*ome days, carp will feed like swine at the slop trough, plowing right over a flat, inhaling seemingly everything in their paths. On other days, they can be as fickle and spooky as permit. I can't tell you how many trout and bonefish guides I've heard tell me how much they respect carp as difficult fish to fool. You can travel throughout the West, for example, and learn that when the guides go fishing on their time off at the end of the day, they're often not casting at trout—they chase carp.

Carp will eat just about anything, from crayfish to Cheetos. That's a good news/ bad news deal. The angler's options are almost limitless, which means the angler has to think hard before choosing a fly to tie on.

They can be found almost anywhere—again, a good news/bad news deal. The good news is that you can fish for carp in an odd assortment of places, from the pristine flats of Lake Michigan to the less-than-bucolic aquascape of the Los Angeles River. The angler must stay sharp, keep his or her eyes peeled, and factor in the less anticipated when they chase carp.

Compare that to the trout river. When the mayflies are hatching, even a novice angler can reasonably guess what to tie on. The rings left by rising trout on the river surface are de facto bull's-eyes that give you a pretty good idea of where to drop the cast. Trout fishing is about understanding systems and patterns. The better you can do that, the better your chances for success. That's also generally true when it comes to bonefish moving on tides, tarpon rolling through channels, or redfish feeding in a marsh—and it's true with carp as well.

The thing is, in carp fishing, those systems and patterns are far more subtle and harder to predict, and they change more frequently than most anglers expect.

Carp can live in environments that few other gamefish will tolerate.
Photo by Tim Romano

Schooling carp. *Photo by Kevin Morlock*

And yet another challenge is that carp are extremely sensitive, communicative fish. They have massive lateral lines, so they can sense danger from a distance. Not only that, they'll also signal that danger to other fish. Oftentimes, I've seen a school of carp slowly cruise into range, and with one errant cast, one awkward slap of the line, not only did I cause the fish I was targeting to flee, but the whole school up and vanished in an instant. Poof.

No fish species connects the sports of angling and hunting better than carp.

Barry Reynolds, Brad Befus, and John Berryman wrote *Carp on the Fly: A Fly-fishing Guide* (with a foreword by Dave Whitlock) more than 15 years ago, and that book has been the standard that got many anglers to embrace the challenge of carp fishing. My dog-eared copy of that book has followed me on many fishing trips, even when I wasn't planning to fish for carp. The basic knowledge that these guys introduced to fly anglers is still very relevant and important. As more anglers have endeavored to chase carp with flies, a few more tips and techniques have come to the fore, and I'll be explaining some of them in this book. But the ultimate lesson a carp angler can learn is that the more one sees and experiences, the more he or she realizes that carp fishing with flies is a labyrinth of challenges that can last more than a lifetime.

Photo by Tim Romano

The Everyman Fish

*O*ne other "why carp" point to make has to do with the issues of access and angling pressure.

The popularity of fly fishing, especially fly fishing for trout, has also had a negative impact on our fisheries. Without getting into a political debate here, we might all acknowledge that the more people there are who fly fish, the more pressure that puts on certain rivers and lakes. It's good to have a larger constituency of people who care about trout and rivers. And where stream access laws allow people to own and control waters, fly fishing for trout has become a pay-to-play situation in some spots. (Believe me, there are still thousands of miles and acres of streams and lakes for the public to enjoy, which is what makes fishing in America the envy of anglers around the world.) Still, not everyone has the money to join the private fishing club, or pay for a guide trip. And not everyone has the funds to jet off to a tropical paradise for some flats fishing.

Carp are the "everyman" fish, and you can make an exotic adventure, and develop your fly-fishing skills, almost anywhere—from the river running through downtown, to the ponds of a municipal golf course, natural lakes, manmade reservoirs, spillways below dams, and on and on.

Are there situations where carp threaten the habitat and compete with other game fish, such as trout? Absolutely. In some places, there are too many carp. Which is all the more reason to fish for them. It's one realm where the fly anglers, and the bait fishermen, and the bowfishing folks can all get along. Carp are more than able to handle any pressures we put on them. There are plenty to go around. And plenty to learn and enjoy by chasing carp.

Facing above: popular streams with public access
are often jammed. *Photo by Michael Frasier*

Facing below: carp are exciting gamefish, no matter
where they live. *Photo by Tim Romano*

Below: even a nearby neighborhood park might offer
good carp fishing. *Photo by Anne Kitzman*

Photo by Tim Romano

Facing: historic drawings of brown trout and carp

A Tale of Two Fishes

*I*n the late 1800s, two fish species were brought from Germany to America. Back then, the first fish was considered a prize. They adorned the ponds of European palaces, and were considered among the most "worthy" and treasured species on the planet, primarily for their heartiness. They were brought to America with the great hope that they could become a viable food source for a growing nation— the answer to a major challenge at a time when native fish stocks had already been depleted in many areas, and refrigerated shipment wasn't possible. Julius A. Poppe brought five of these fish to California in 1872, and within 4 years, they had proliferated into a successful fish-farming operation. Then, in 1877, the U.S. Fish Commission initiated a major effort to cultivate these fish throughout the country. The first government shipment from Europe was deemed so valuable that the fish were guarded around the clock after they had been planted in Druid Hill ponds near Baltimore, and efforts to transport and plant these fish in other carefully selected waters throughout the country were carried out with painstaking precision.

The second fish—also a prized species—was introduced into the Baldwin River in

Michigan in April 1884. This fish was held in high esteem more for its "sporting" characteristics than any widespread commercial potential. But this fish couldn't just be dumped anywhere. Comparatively speaking, this fish was fragile, requiring relatively cool, clean waters with ample natural food sources (like insects and other aquatic invertebrates) in order to survive, let alone reproduce.

Flash forward to the present day, and the contrast of where these two fish species—the common carp (fish one) and the brown trout (fish two)—ended up in terms of "social status" in the eyes of anglers is remarkable. The carp took hold in American waters immediately, and within a few decades, had multiplied with such success in a wide range of waters that by the turn of the 20th Century, they were already considered a nuisance species.

Brown trout, on the other hand, are revered to this day as the very foundation of fly-fishing culture in America, despite the fact that browns aren't "native" to any American waters (or the rivers in countries throughout the world like Chile, Argentina, New Zealand, Australia, and South Africa, where they were also introduced). Anglers also sometimes overlook the fact that the brown trout essentially "kicked out" some native trout species from various watersheds by outcompeting them— eating them and their food, and reproducing more efficiently than, say, brook trout in Michigan or certain cutthroat trout species in the American West.

Brown trout. *Photo by Matt Guymon*

Still, one of the most effective grassroots conservation organizations in the United States, Trout Unlimited, of which I am proudly a member (partly because I learned to fly fish on the Baldwin River and am still very much enamored of brown trout) was established in 1959, not far from where those brown trout were first planted. TU's mission, while primarily focused on native salmonid species, still supports significant efforts to preserve and protect those cold, clean waters where the relatively fragile *Salmo trutta* swim. Brown trout will never be native fish, but anglers have adopted the reverent euphemism "wild fish" to describe their beloved browns—at least those that weren't reared in a fish hatchery.

Carp, on the other hand, well they're considered "invasive species," which is perhaps a by-product of their own genetic superiority. There is no "Carp Unlimited" because this über-fish doesn't need any help. The carp has suffered the same stigma of the working class, blue-collar human immigrants who worked

Above: common carp
Photo by John Bartlett

Left: Asian carp
Photo by Armondo Martinez

the docks, cleared the fields, and built the transcontinental railroad, while the brown trout fell into favor with the genteel, sporting elite. The carp is a draft horse, while the brown trout is a thoroughbred.

And no doubt, in some places, carp are making a harsh impact on rivers and lakes. The threat that Asian carp (a name that envelops many species, like silver carp and bighead carp) pose to the Great Lakes is one of the most significant pending environmental catastrophes of our time. Yes, there are many situations where carp species of all sorts should be eradicated if at all possible, in order to preserve American fisheries.

But to call the common carp "invasive" while holding the brown trout in high esteem is a bit unfair. They're both immigrants.

Photo by Kevin Morlock

Carp Biology 101

I'm including three types of carp in this book: common carp, mirror carp, and grass carp. Common carp are by far the most, well, common species anglers encounter in American lakes and rivers. Mirror carp are a subspecies of common carp, so named because their scales are oblong and shiny, akin to small mirrors. While they are genetically slightly different from common carp, and vary dramatically in appearance, they generally share the same biology, habits, and so forth. The techniques an angler uses to chase mirror carp are by and large the same as those used to catch common carp with flies. It's the same game.

Grass carp, on the other hand, are strictly vegetarian, and thus provide a much more limited (and challenging) opportunity to catch with flies. But they are no less wonderful fighters, and frequently will jump after being hooked. Grass carp perhaps represent the "pinnacle" of challenge for a carp angler. I've written more specifically on grass carp in Chapter 25 of this book. (Perhaps as if to suggest, "Now that you've got a handle on the common carp challenge, if you really want to frustrate yourself, here's how to chase grass carp.") For now, assume that what you're reading is based on common carp and grass carp.

The common carp (*Cyprinus carpio* of the family Cyprinidae) is native to the Caspian Sea region of south-central Asia, though various subspecies are thought to have evolved in other geographic areas, from the Danube River in Europe to southeast Asia. They have been transplanted (sometimes illegally) throughout the world. In fact, they are considered among the world's top 100 invasive species, according to the Global Invasive Species Database.

Carp earned this dubious distinction because they can live almost anywhere. Why is it that the goldfish (a type of carp) lives in the fishbowls of so many young children? Exactly . . . because they're hard to kill. You don't need to meticulously balance the pH levels in the aquarium, add a bubble wand to oxygenate the water,

Mirror carp. *Photo by Kirk Deeter*

or keep that water in a narrow temperature range. The fishbowl just needs to have water that's one thing—wet—for a goldfish to be able to survive in it.

It's basically the same deal with common carp in the wild.

Carp prefer fairly temperate waters (in the 60s and 70s Fahrenheit), but they can tolerate a wide range of temperatures and water conditions. They can survive in lakes that freeze in winter, as well as in rivers and sloughs that can warm to over 90 degrees Fahrenheit. Only when waters approach the 100-degree mark will carp die—and that's long after most other freshwater fish species would be long gone.

Carp can survive in moving currents (rivers) as well as in calm, even stagnant, ponds. The carp's ability to survive and reproduce in relatively confined spaces is one attribute that has made it desirable for fish farming operations for centuries.

A carp's lifespan is among the longest of any fish. Some carp have been documented to have lived for 50 years or longer, though the average lifespan of the average carp, of course, depends on water conditions, the presence of predators, food availability, and other factors.

Carp "breathe" primarily with their gills, naturally, but they also have the ability to gulp air by breaching the surface and literally sucking in air with their mouths. This is another factor that helps them persist in stagnant, less oxygenated waters.

They are also prolific breeders. The optimal water temperatures for carp to spawn are in the mid-60s Fahrenheit (not less than 62 degrees), and a typical adult female can spawn three or four times in a given year, laying as many as 300,000 eggs each time.

Carp gulping air

Photo above by Tim Roman

Photo at left by Brian Johns

The Characteristics and Senses of Carp

6

*C*arp are built like piscine linebackers, thick-bodied and with powerful tails that allow them to accelerate to speeds that top 10 miles per hour. This might not sound all that fast, but that's equivalent to trout, and in a moving current, can make for quite the force on the other end of a fly line. They can grow as long as 4 feet, and reach nearly 100 pounds. The largest carp ever caught by an angler was hooked on Lac de Curton (Rainbow Lake) near Bordeaux, France, and weighed 94 pounds. Rainbow Lake is world-renowned as a carp destination for conventional-tackle anglers, who will set up their "bivvies" (bivouacs) to camp, chum, cast, and hopefully hook a large fish.

Carp are among the fastest-growing fish in freshwater, able to reach double-digit weights in a matter of months—again, depending on food source and environment. But a distinctive, mature fish can achieve celebrity status in parts of Europe. I'm not kidding. In 2009, for example, the carp angling world literally mourned the death (apparently as a result of ingesting uncooked, toxic "Tiger Nuts" bait) of Benson, a 25-year-old female common carp that had been caught 63 times and had an estimated worth of 20,000 British pounds. (Google "Benson and fish" and you'll see; I couldn't make this stuff up if I tried.)

Carp are typically golden, bronze, olive green, and/or brown in color, depending on the food they eat and the environment in which they live. They have thick, armorlike scales along their sides and backs; long, serrated, and spiny dorsal fins; broad tails; and sweeping pectoral and anal fins on their softer, lighter bellies. The scales and fins of carp often exhibit bright red and black hues.

Perhaps the trademark feature of a common carp is its round, hoselike mouth—hence the nickname Ol' Rubberlips—that tilts downward to allow the fish to vacuum food off the bottoms of lakes or rivers. Note that the downward slope of

Carp grow to trophy proportions. *Photo by Trevor Tanner*

a carp's mouth is thought to be the product of domestication; wilder carp, which are more prone to chase different food types and feed less on the bottom, have less of a drop.

Common carp, unlike the goldfish in the bowl, also have barbels—whiskerlike organs that extend from either side of their snouts. These sensory organs contain taste buds, allowing the fish to swim in murky water and taste their way along, sorting out preferred food from other stuff along the way. There are also taste

A. caudal fin – B. dorsal fin – C. lateral line – D. nostril – E. barbel
F. operculum – G. pectoral fin – H. pelvic fin – I. vent – J. anal fin

Photo by John Hendrickson

buds on the carp's anal and pectoral fins. The insides of carp mouths also have special cells that can distinguish one taste from another—perhaps even lock into memory "good tastes" from bad ones, such as the metal of a fishhook. Many serious carp anglers, conventional or fly, will tell you that it's difficult enough to hook a carp in the first place, but it's especially hard to catch any carp a second time. One of the leading theories about why that is holds that carp have such refined senses of taste and smell that they'll burn the bad experience of being caught into instinct, associating the smells and tastes of that syrup-soaked bait, and hook—or the sight and taste of a fly—as they do so.

I don't know for certain that carp can "memorize" danger scents, tastes, or smells, but I do know that they are tremendously difficult to fool more than once. Among fish, carp might best represent the old adage, "Fool me once, shame on you; fool me twice, shame on me."

Kevin Morlock—who owns Indigo Guide Service in Michigan, and along with guide Steve Martinez has recently turned anglers onto the remarkable, carp-based, flats-fishing experience to be had off Beaver Island in Lake Michigan—recently told me that he had tagged 300 carp in the past few years, and has re-caught only six of those fish.

FIND OUT MORE ABOUT INDIGO GUIDE SERVICE

Carp also have a keen sense of smell. Scientific studies have shown that carp can actually distinguish the amino acids in certain food sources, such as crustaceans, worms, vegetation, and so forth. Along with their superior sense of taste, a carp's ability to smell different foods also helps the fish live and eat in dirty waters.

HINT: GETTING CHUMMY

Much of traditional carp fishing with bait and tackle revolves around chumming, specifically because carp depend so highly on their senses of smell and taste. Serious tournament anglers all have their favorite "glugs" and syrups, and mixing up chum recipes and delivering them by "spod" catapult (or even remote-controlled boat) is an artform. Most fly anglers would not dunk their Woolly Buggers in worm juice. I'm not suggesting you step over that line when you're carp fishing, but if ever there were a species and situation where a little chum or scent wouldn't seem quite so disreputable—you're "slumming" when you carp fish anyway—this is it.

Just because carp don't need to see in order to eat doesn't mean that they have compromised vision. In fact, carp have keen vision when compared to other fish, and if you've seen how they react to motions and shadows in clear water (carp also love clear water), you'll know just how well they can see. Scientists believe that carp have the ability to sense different colors as well.

Lastly, carp have a seemingly uncanny sense of hearing. While some of that ability is attributed to the fact that carp have large lateral lines that sense vibrations in the water, it's worth noting that carp also have "ears." They can detect sound frequencies from 60 to 6,000 Hz. Their ears are comprised of otoliths, which are tiny sacs connected to a small bone. Another elaborate series of bones and sinewy matter called the Weberian apparatus connects the ears with the fish's swim bladder. The net result serves as an amplifier of sorts, allowing carp to hear things many other fish wouldn't notice.

Photo by Kevin Morlock

Photo by Michael Frasier

Carp can survive even in stagnant water.
Photo by Tim Romano

Where Carp Live

7

*A*s mentioned, carp can survive in many types of water and water conditions, except for saltwater. An ideal carp environment typically has significant vegetation—carp will actually eat live and decaying plant matter, and they like to use plants as cover to hide from predators. The more vegetation, the more other food sources such as insects and baitfish will abound as well.

While carp tolerate various water temperatures, they prefer temperate waters (60–80 degrees Fahrenheit) and will actively seek out certain areas specifically because of water temperatures. Carp like to find warm (but not hot) water. An angler will often find carp on the sun-heated flats, and above the thermocline (the level where the temperature changes, from warm to cold, as one descends) in deep lakes. It's possible to see and hook carp in water 20 feet deep in some places—like the Great Lakes—but you'll usually encounter carp in shallower water.

As with many fish species, carp also gravitate to currents, drop-offs, and structure. But unlike other types of fish, the carp's patterns are often unpredictable. They might be working a mudflat one day, and cruising a ledge in open, deeper water the next. Whether they're keyed on different food sources, or the weather forces those changes, it's hard to know for sure. That's why it's imperative for a serious carp angler to spend plenty of time observing carp, as well as casting at carp. You want your bag of tricks to be as deep as possible. And though I hate to admit it, no book or magazine story, or online blog post or report, will sync you up with the specific intricacies of the carp waters you fish better than your own experiences and observations ultimately will.

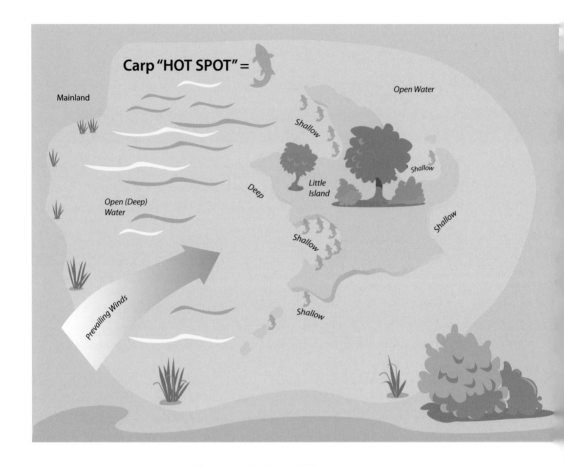

Illustration by Mary Kelley

Denny Breer, the late, great trout fishing master of Utah's Green River, once shared a simple, one-line axiom with me that I think perfectly sums up the angler's learning curve. He said: "Time on water equals fish." And I've yet to meet a seasoned angler—be that on the tarpon flats of Florida, the salmon rivers in Alaska, or even the dorado streams in the heart of the South American jungle—who didn't agree.

Personal experience trumps all. And that's especially true when it comes to carp fishing.

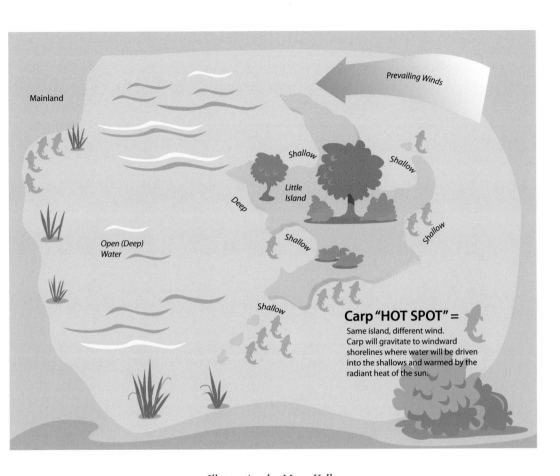

Illustration by Mary Kelley

Common carp (*Cyrpinus carpio*)
Photo by DPM

How Carp Behave

8

*C*arp are "social" fish. As Reynolds, Befus, and Berryman pointed out in *Carp on the Fly,* they are more prone to "shoaling" behavior (which means they hang out in packs) than true "schooling" (which means they swim in the same direction). I firmly believe that carp work in unison, testing certain areas, exploring others, and functioning as a team if you will, not only to find feeding opportunities, but to flee as a group when even one fish senses danger.

Many times have I stood on the edge of a flat on Lake Michigan, where the carp scene played out as having one fish—seemingly a "sentry"—come cruising up out of the deeper, open water onto the flat, and within several yards of where I was stationed, totally still. The fish circled away and out toward the deep water, but if I remained exactly where I was, completely motionless, within a matter of a few minutes, I'd spot three or four carp come cruising into view, sweeping roughly the same pattern that the first fish had, before circling back away and vanishing into the deeper water. I'd spend another few minutes waiting almost motionless, and sure enough, 40 or more fish came lumbering along that same circuit the previous fish had followed, and they all set up shop and started feeding on the flat. Until, that is, I made an errant cast, which spooked the fish nearest to me, and ultimately sent the whole group packing.

If I had seen this only once, I would have chalked it up as an odd phenomenon, but I've seen this same thing happen over and over, particularly when fishing on larger lakes.

Much of the carp's social behavior is attributed to pheromones, or chemicals that the carp secrete into the water, that are sensed by other carp to trigger certain responses, like "alarm," or "follow me to the food," or "hey baby, let's go spawn."

Schooling carp. *Photo by Kevin Morlock*

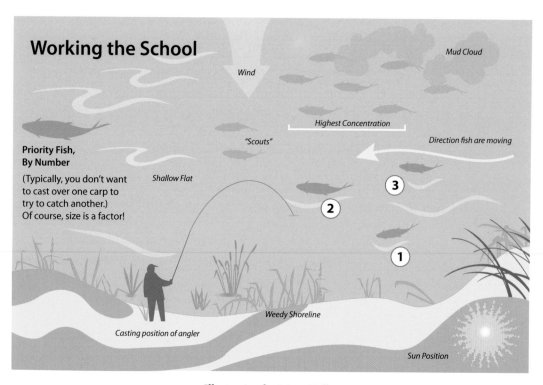

Working the School

Mud Cloud

Wind

Highest Concentration

"Scouts"

Direction fish are moving

Priority Fish, By Number

(Typically, you don't want to cast over one carp to try to catch another.) Of course, size is a factor!

Shallow Flat

3

2

1

Weedy Shoreline

Casting position of angler

Sun Position

Illustration by Mary Kelley

Interestingly, Jean-Paul (J.P.) Lipton, the mastermind behind the blog rough fisher.com (with whom I have had the pleasure to fish for carp on several occasions, learning something new every time) has a theory that carp in rivers often behave differently than carp in lakes, because the pheromone signals secreted in the water are more quickly washed away in moving currents. So, for example, the reason a group of carp might get spooked by your presence on a river, but then return and "reset" as they were after only a few minutes, while the carp you spook in a lake might be gone for hours or even days, is because the pheromone signals have washed downstream in the river, while they linger in the lake. That's interesting food for thought when you consider various angling approaches that come into play on different types of water.

FIND OUT MORE ABOUT ROUGHFISHER

Erin Block releases a carp. *Photo by Jay Zimmerman*

Lakes, Ponds, and Rivers

9

*T*he good news, as I've already said, is that you can find carp in just about any body of fresh water. The bad news is that there are substantial differences in how you should fly fish for carp in those different types of water. River carp are different from pond carp, and pond carp are different from big-lake carp.

I'll give you some more examples.

I've heard and read stories by many anglers whom I respect dearly, claiming that a "cruising carp," working its way through the water is, in fact, not a ripe target. We'll get more into the motions and postures of carp as they swim later on. But when I see a carp in Grand Traverse Bay on Lake Michigan, for example, my angling senses go into overdrive. Seeing a fish that's come up from deeper water, and is now slinking along the shoreline, is exactly the scenario I'm hoping for.

It might be a little less true on a smaller lake or pond. I remember one afternoon when Charlie Meyers of the Denver Post and I had met up with this young buck outdoor writer and self-professed carp junkie named Will Rice, at Jackson Lake near Ft. Morgan, Colorado. It was May, and Will had scouted a massive group of carp tailing in the mud flats on the eastern edge of the lake a few days before—which got him pumped up enough to make a call to Charlie—who in turn was pumped up enough to call his buddy from *Field & Stream* (me). This was my first introduction to Will, and to this day, while Charlie—who had been a mentor to both Will and me—sadly is no longer around, Will remains one of my best fishing buddies and carp "confidants."

Will had promised that Jackson was going to "go off," and it did. But while Will and I lashed away with casts, chasing the golden tails that glinted in the sunlight on the high plains, Charlie simply waded out carefully to a spot where he stood knee-deep and waited. The fish collectively worked a circular pattern. Even as they passed his position, Charlie simply held tight, and didn't bother casting. I

41

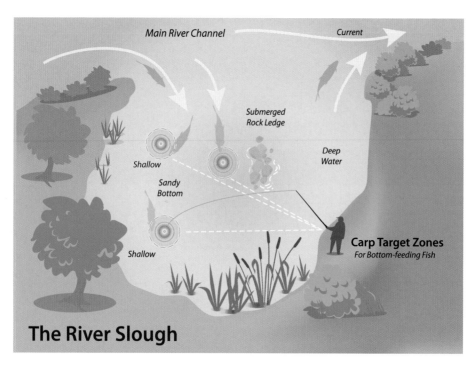

Main River Channel

Current

Submerged
Rock Ledge

Deep
Water

Shallow

Sandy
Bottom

Shallow

Carp Target Zones
For Bottom-feeding Fish

The River Slough

Illustrations by Mary Kelley

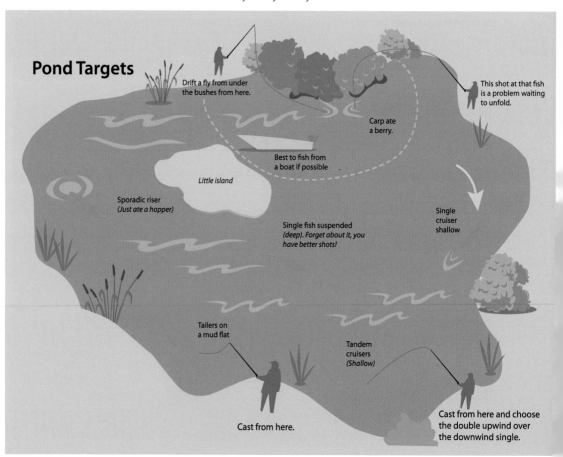

Pond Targets

Drift a fly from under
the bushes from here.

This shot at that fish
is a problem waiting
to unfold.

Carp ate
a berry.

Best to fish from
a boat if possible   .

Little island

Sporadic riser
(Just ate a hopper)

Single fish suspended
(deep). Forget about it, you
have better shots!

Single
cruiser
shallow

Tailers on
a mud flat

Tandem
cruisers
(Shallow)

Cast from here.

Cast from here and choose
the double upwind over
the downwind single.

Feeding carp. *Photo by Kevin Morlock*

wondered what he was thinking at the time. But I also noticed that, as Charlie patiently waited, the wakes of cruising fish yielded to tails and boils. In other words, the carp stopped, and started to eat off the bottom. And then, only then, did Charlie unfurl his pinpoint cast, and drop his rusty Woolly Bugger in the near vicinity of a fish that wasn't any more than 30 feet away. That carp ate the fly, as did the next, and the next that Charlie was wise enough to wait out and allow to transition from moving to eating.

In rivers, we often see trout in riffles, as well as in the runs and glides downstream from the riffles. All those trout in all those places warrant attention, and some casts. You'll find carp in all those areas, also. But in my experience, it's the fish at the head of the riffle, and well-anchored in the glide—especially if they're fairly stationary and tilted downward, eating, that deserve the most attention. You can indeed hook a carp with a nymph by dragging that fly through the run now and then, but the "players" are typically in the skinny, slower water.

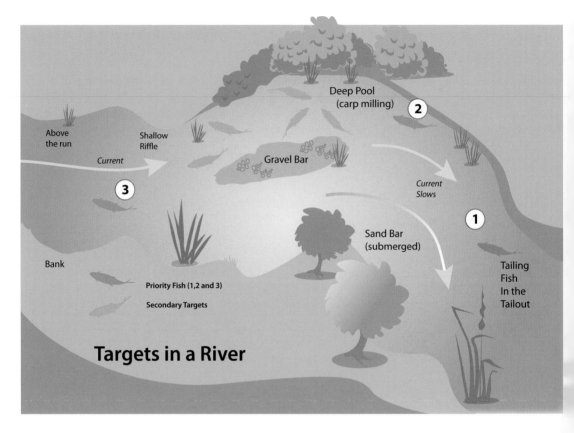

Deep Pool
(carp milling)   ②

Above
the run   Shallow
                 Riffle
        Current   Gravel Bar
                                              ③   Current
                                                       Slows
                                                              ①

                          Sand Bar
Bank   (submerged)   Tailing
                                                      Fish
            Priority Fish (1,2 and 3)   In the
            Secondary Targets   Tailout

Targets in a River

Illustration by Mary Kelley

Of course, this all differs from place to place, and in different conditions.

The mighty Columbia River, for example, is probably one of the top five carp destinations in America. Ten-pound-plus fish thrive there in remarkable numbers, and an angler who knows what he or she is doing can have legitimate shots at 20-pounders from March through October. John Bartlett, who runs the blog carponthefly.blogspot.com, has earned his stripes the hard way. It took him months to figure out that carp in that river are keyed on clams. Clams don't swim fast and far. There, it's all about putting a fly in the "zone," and waiting the carp out, hoping that they'll pick it up. Different river, different scenario.

So give yourself a reason to fish the way you do. Understand why the carp are in certain waters, be that in a large lake, a pond, or a river, and you've cut the guessing game in half. More often than not, the key to understanding why carp are where they are has to do with understanding what they're eating, and why.

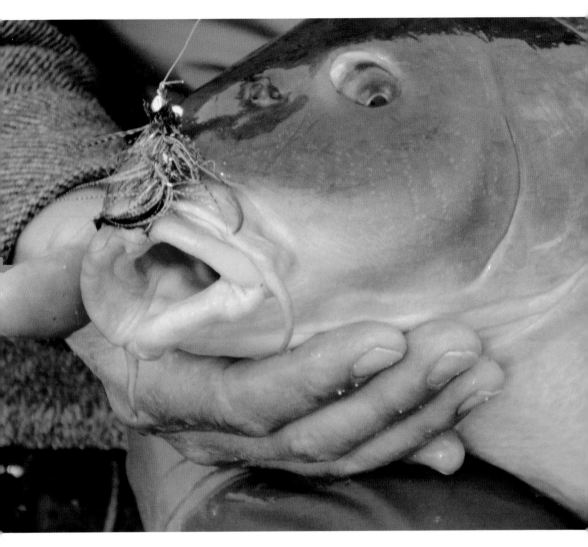

Photo by Kirk Deeter

Photo by Kirk Deeter

What Carp Eat

10

*A*nother good news/bad news situation: The good news is that carp are omnivores, meaning they eat just about anything, including baitfish, worms, crayfish, vegetation, seeds, berries, insects, potato chips, cigarette butts, and more.

The bad news is that carp are omnivores, meaning they eat just about anything, including baitfish, worms, crayfish, vegetation, seeds, berries, insects, potato chips, cigarette butts, and more.

This is no exaggeration: I know guides who fish for carp on Lake Las Vegas with flies made of bright orange foam ear plugs. Yes, carp are curious fish and they will react often to bright colors, but the real reason this fly works—and apparently works well—is that the orange floating blobs resemble the crumbs of Cheetos and other snack foods that end up in the lake. Does this make a carp a "sucker" for anything that's edible and falls in the water, or is the carp smart enough to adapt to a food source? You decide.

The bread-and-butter food for carp in many places is the crayfish, so flies that are brown, rust, or olive in color, and can be danced around the bottom will often attract a bite. Carp also love to eat worms (annelids), clams, snails, leeches, and so forth. When I'm fishing a carp lake for the very first time, and I know there are crayfish in that water, I will often start with a crayfish pattern. But no matter where I am—big lake, small pond, or river—I always carry a healthy supply of red- and burgundy-colored worm flies. The San Juan Worm—a staple trout pattern—is a good start, but I love the undulating action of a loose-tail worm tied sparsely to the hook.

Actually, before I pick any fly, I'll really start by sitting on the bank and watching the water, hopefully spotting a few fish, and trying to figure out what they are eating before I make a cast at all.

Start by watching the water carefully for signs of feeding fish.
Photo by Kyle Perkins

One of the biggest mistakes newbie carp anglers (many of whom are converts from the trout realm) make is to assume that trout are the only fish that key on insects. Carp, like walleyes, bass, and other fish, make insects a major part of their diets. Aquatic midges, mayflies, caddis, crane flies, dragonflies, damselflies, waterbugs, stoneflies, and scuds, as well as terrestrials such as grasshoppers, crickets, inchworms, ants, and beetles, are all preferred food sources for many fish other than trout, and that certainly includes carp. Moreover, carp are apt to key on various stages of these insects, be they nymphs, drakes, or spinners (mayflies). As when trout fishing, understanding what hatches happen where and when can be critically valuable information when fishing for carp.

One prevailing theory is that carp are not terribly inclined to eat baitfish like minnows, shad, and so forth. And that's probably true in many waters. However, remember that carp are the ultimate adaptors and opportunists, and they'll eat whatever they can to fuel their bodies. The carp in the Great Lakes, for example,

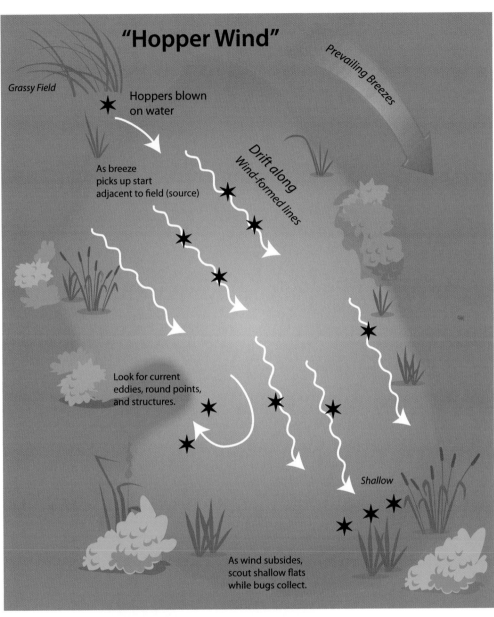

"Hopper Wind"

Grassy Field

Hoppers blown on water

Prevailing Breezes

Drift along Wind-formed lines

As breeze picks up start adjacent to field (source)

Look for current eddies, round points, and structures.

Shallow

As wind subsides, scout shallow flats while bugs collect.

Illustration above by Mary Kelley

Carp feed on a wide variety of aquatic and terrestrial insects.
Photo by Kevin Morlock

Goby

have taken a particular shine to eating the invasive goby fish that are found in many rocky shoals and flats. While this is a relatively new phenomenon in the course of natural history (heck, the common carp being in the Great Lakes at all is a relatively new phenomenon in the grand scheme of things), carp are acutely in tune and aware of the protein rewards to be had by sucking down those unfortunate gobies, so baitfish patterns (like a white Zonker, or a Gummy Minnow) can work well in those places. It's all about understanding what's on the menu in any given place, at any given time.

Carp will also eat plant matter, like mulberries, cottonseeds, even wildflowers and weeds, as well as vegetation that grows beneath the water's surface. When you see carp rising under a mulberry bush, you needn't stretch your imagination too much to figure out what they're eating. When the wind is blowing and grasshoppers are flying, put two and two together to make an educated guess. You'll never be 100 percent certain, but you'll have a solid hunch, and in the end, when it comes to guessing what carp are eating at any given time, the best you can do is play the odds and trust your hunches.

How Carp Eat

11

*O*bserving how carp eat will often tell you as much about what they're eating as the natural telltales (like bugs floating on the surface) ever will. When anglers take the time to watch the fish actually eat, they can shorten the learning curve dramatically, and limit the trial-and-error casts that inevitably spook more carp than they hook.

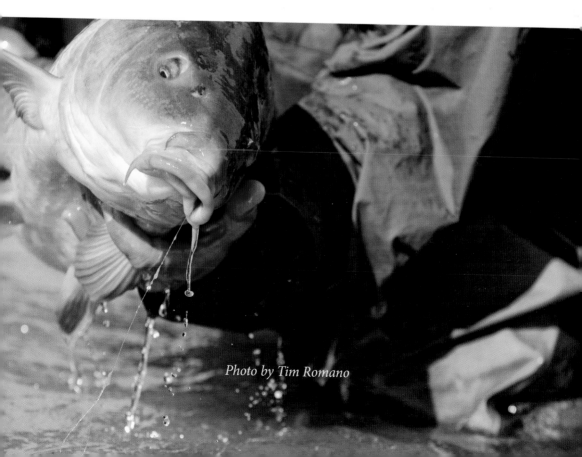

Photo by Tim Romano

Fish rooting around on the bottom, for example, are actively feeding, probably on those types of foods that live on the bottom, such as crayfish, snails, worms, and so on. But take that one step further and ask yourself whether the fish are rooting around on a gravel or sandy bottom (in which case you know they're eating animals) or if they're eating in the weeds, in which case they might be eating the plants themselves, but are more likely slurping down aquatic insects that live among the vegetation.

Then again, you also must factor in how your fly will work in that feeding environment. For example, what's typically going to happen when you drag a weighted nymph or crayfish pattern through a bed of cabbage on the bottom of a lake? It's going to wind up coated in green slime, and look unappetizing (or at least not like a nymph or a crayfish) after just one cast. Perhaps it's better in those situations to suspend a nymph off a dry fly floating on the surface, or twitch a soft-hackle fly ever so gently into view of the carp.

Finally, there are also times when you can tease a carp into biting an attractor fly—a pattern that doesn't really look like any natural creature, but is just ugly, gaudy, and irritating enough to pique the curiosity of an interested carp.

Let the fish tell you what to tie on, and how to present it, and your success rate will improve incrementally.

We're going to talk more about specific flies and fishing situations in a bit.

HINT: DETECTING STRIKES

One common difficulty many novice carp anglers have is detecting a strike. Sometimes, the fish simple inhales a fly without moving its head in a way that you'd notice. There are a few ways around that. First, when you're stripping a fly like a streamer or nymph, keep it moving until you feel the resistance. Don't stop that fly when a carp moves toward it. Motion is what got the fish's attention in the first place. With dry flies and plant flies, or small nymphs suspended in the water column, you might also think about putting the fly an inch or two off center, meaning not directly under the carp's nose. That requires a move you'll notice in order for the carp to eat the fly.

Carp feed close to scum lines. *Photo by Kyle Perkins*

Photo by Kevin Morlock

A slight chop on the surface can help make it
more difficult for carp to spot you.
Photo by Kevin Morlock

On Weather and Water Conditions 12

*T*here are other factors that an angler simply cannot control, yet they come into play every time you go fishing. Things like weather, wind, and water clarity play a huge role in fly fishing, especially fly fishing for carp.

In speaking with other fly anglers who chase carp, I hear "perfect carp conditions" nearly always described the same way. Clear skies with sunshine, and clear water, with no wind, or perhaps a slight breeze to add a very light chop to the surface (which helps camouflage the angler and his/her casts), is usually the best-case scenario for spotting fish. And when it comes to fly fishing for carp, seeing the fish is more than half the battle.

It's important to note that carp do feed in all seasons, and while water temperatures often dictate whether they'll be found in deeper or shallower water (deeper in the heat of summer, shallower in the shoulder seasons when carp are searching for warmer water in which to eat or spawn), the savvy carp angler is usually focused on finding where warm water has been pushed up against a shallow shoreline.

When the wind blows too hard, it can stir up the water, reducing visibility, and making long, accurate casts with a fly line all the more difficult. Then again, a steady breeze can be the carp angler's best friend, especially on open lakes. The wind pushes the water into shallow coves and bays where the sun heats it, and the carp inevitably follow. It's important to know the direction of the wind, and focus your efforts on those windward shorelines, rather than fishing a lee shore, where the water is often pushed out to mix with deeper, cooler currents.

As far as weather fronts, barometric pressure, rain, snow, and so forth go, carp are so unpredictable and fickle that it's hard to peg when the fishing is going to heat up or not, solely on what's falling from the sky or not. I've had epic carp days in a light mist, when the clouds limited my ability to spot fish other than those tailing in the shallows. I've never had much luck in a driving rainstorm or snowstorm. But then again, I've reached the point in my angling pursuits that I don't personally like to try all that hard in conditions when the wind is blowing 30 miles an hour and the sleet is sticking to my eyelids.

In short, if you see clear, calm days in the forecast—whether that's in April or July—those are usually the best days for carpin'. But don't be afraid to experiment in all conditions.

Fish a windward shoreline whenever possible.
Photo by Kevin Morlock

Why Carp Are Hard to Catch with Flies

13

So, let's factor in all these things. We know that carp have supreme senses, better than most fish. They eat by smell, which isn't much good to a fly angler, because most flies don't smell like anything but steel, fur, and feathers. I suppose you can "glug" your flies with the syrupy goos and scents that Euro-style carp anglers use, but most American fly-angling purists would consider that cheating. The scent issue does, however, raise the concern of how other substances the angler handles—such as fly floatant, sunscreen, bug spray, and so on—could ultimately end up on the fly, tippet, and leader, and thereby come into play when you drop that pattern in front of the carp.

We know also that carp feed by sense of taste. Again, no help to the fly angler, since most of the flies I stick in my mouth as I'm tying on a new tippet taste like fur, feathers, and metal, or maybe stale foam.

We know that carp can feed by sight, which is a good thing (maybe the only good thing) fly anglers have going for them. Then again, because carp have decent vision, we have to worry that the carp might see us, our lines, or our casts. And if the fly looks at all "wrong," that will be a deal breaker, too.

A carp's incredible ability to hear sounds and sense vibrations is another glitch. We must be super-careful not to grind our boots on gravel, or clunk around in the boat, if we really want the best opportunity to sneak up on a carp and make a cast and presentation that will fool the fish.

We know carp can live in a wide range of environments, and that they eat many different things. Hmmmm. That's not much help when it comes to finding the fish, and picking the right fly to toss at them.

And lastly, we know that if we make one little mistake, triggering a bad reaction in any of a carp's senses, that fish is not only going to split the scene, he or she is going to tell all his or her friends and take them along.

We must be crazy.

Then again, if we're actually able to pull it off, and trick a carp with a fly, we know we've tackled one of angling's greatest challenges. Fortunately, there are a number of tricks and tips that can help us do just that.

Conway Bowman releases a nice carp. *Photo by Al Quattrocchi*

Photo by Kevin Morlock

Photo by Jay Zimmerman

PART TWO · PLAYING THE GAME

Photo by Cameron Mortenson

Gear: Rods, Reels, Lines, Leaders, Tippet, Waders, and More

14

RODS

As with any type of fly fishing, the gear you use is a purely subjective consideration. What I like might not fit your style, and what you like might not flip my switch. The most high-tech, expensive rod in the world will never offer the advantages of a pure casting stroke and the ability to anticipate fish behavior, and those things happen only through time spent on the water. Gear should never be a crutch. And gear should never be blamed for poor results.

I have caught carp on fly rods ranging from a 4-weight fiberglass model (purely by accident) to a 13-foot, 8-weight two-handed Spey rod (with a Babine double egg fly on a pond in Denver—that one was intended as a joke, until it actually worked).

But my favorite all-around carp stick is a 9-foot, 7-weight, fast-action graphite rod. There are dozens of different manufacturers and models to choose from, and they're all great for different reasons.

I think it's important to have a designated carp rod that you feel comfortable with in a variety of conditions and situations, because the carp-fishing world is so varied and complex that an angler could go broke by buying different rods to fit every specific carp scenario. It's best to find a good all-around rod that you can work in the calm and wind, on rivers and lakes, with big flies and small flies, and so on. Versatility is my key factor in rod selection when it comes to carp, and for me, that has centered on the 9-foot 7-weight.

Now, having said that, of course there are situations where you might want to mix things up, and that's fine also. If you're lake fishing for smaller carp and throwing dry flies from a boat, for example, you might opt for a 10-foot, 6-weight. If you're chasing the big beasts along the windy shorelines of Lake Michigan, a 9-foot, 9-weight (or even 10-weight) might work best.

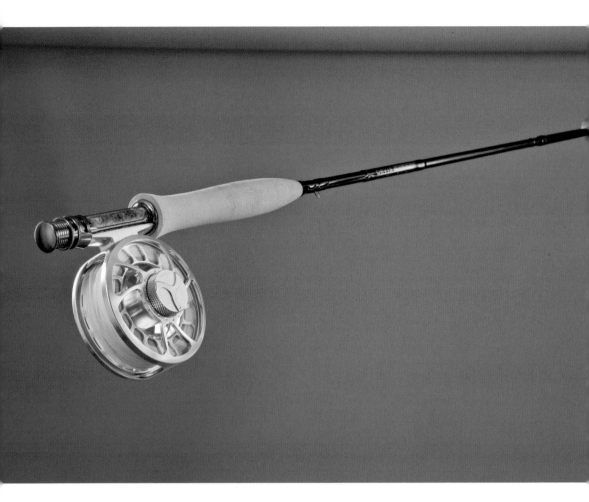

Above and facing photos courtesy of The Orvis Company

A lot of anglers lean toward a 9-foot, 8-weight (the typical bonefishing rod) because carp fishing is very similar to chasing bonefish in that you're often casting heavy flies in the wind, and with luck, pulling in fish that weigh 10 pounds or more. I like a 7-weight because I tend to fish a lot of nymph patterns and small streamers for carp, and I like the added sensitivity that allows me to detect the subtle take.

The bottom line is that the choice is purely up to you. My advice is to find one "baseline" rod model that matches up with your casting style, as well as the conditions, the types of flies, and average size of fish you are most likely to experience on a regular basis, and build your carp-fishing skills around it. If you choose to branch out to different situation-specific rods and rigs as you dabble more with carp, that's great.

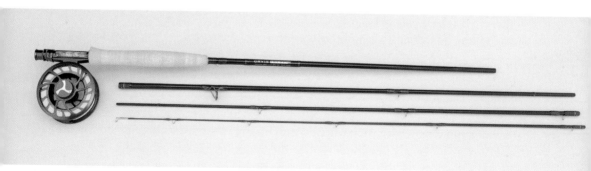

Photo courtesy of The Orvis Company

REELS

Reel performance is important in carp fishing. In most trout-fishing situations, to be brutally honest, the reel's true value is no more than as a spool to hold an angler's line. I don't see my backing knot on a regular basis when I am trout fishing for sub-20-inch fish on a river, and when I do, that usually means I've made a mistake.

With carp, as with bonefish, permit, and other saltwater species, that initial run can be an impressive sprint. Carp don't always make the 100-yard dash like a bonefish, but they can when they want to, especially in certain water conditions, such as a wide-open flat adjacent to deep water. Perhaps more important, carp are inclined to make sudden bursts, stops, and starts during the fight. It's often an unpredictable wrestling match with carp. The saltwater species equivalent is, in my mind, redfish. They tug, they stall; they peel out line and swerve; they run at you, and away from you. For that reason, having a reel with a smooth disk drag—one that's particularly even on the startup, minus hiccups, catches, and jitters—is important.

I fish a disk-drag-equipped, corrosion-resistant, aluminum reel because it's a low-maintenance option, preferably with a reliable sealed drag that works equally well in cold and hot weather. I've fished a number of different reels (and pulled on many with motorcycles, ATVs, and other things to test how smoothly they start on that initial acceleration), and there are many solid options available.

Again, it's a subjective consideration. The real question is what feels comfortable in your hands (by way of the handle, drag adjustment, and so on), and what balances the rod you're casting best. And budget is always a consideration. Don't be talked into spending several hundred dollars for a disk drag reel. Some of those models are heirlooms in the making, but you can find solid drag performance for a couple hundred bucks.

LINES

I use weight-forward, floating lines 99.9 percent of the time when I am fishing for carp.

Let's call it like it is: one of the great appeals of carp is the ability to sight-fish in skinny water. In my opinion, casting heavy sink tips and dredging deep water with big flies should be reserved for species like striped bass, steelhead, tuna, and pike, in situations where they can't be caught any other way. Carp are so often readily available in shallow water that, to me, it doesn't make a whole lot of sense to ply the depths with a specialized fly line to hook one. That's not to say it cannot or should not happen. Sometimes, for example, in the heat of August, when the

Great Lakes carp migrate to deeper water, you might want to cast a sink-tip to catch them. What I'm saying here is that the vast majority of fly fishing for carp can happen with the standard weight-forward, floating line.

There are, however, a number of specialty variations of floating lines to consider. Naturally, the first consideration is to match the weight of your line with the rod you use. There are also variations in tapers of floating lines—some are meant to cast heavy flies, some are designed to help anglers make distance casts, some to make delicate presentations, and so on. Choose a line that helps you cast as heavy a fly as far and as effectively as possible. You don't want to handcuff yourself with a line that can throw a cannonball, but isn't accurate outside of 30 feet. Likewise, you don't want a line that can throw a feather 100 feet, but won't roll within 25 feet. You also want a line that will land with a whisper, rather than a thud, as carp are notoriously spooky when it comes to splashy fly presentations. There are a number of decent options out there, and your own best choice is, well, entirely up to you.

Some other factors to consider are line flexibility and memory. If you are fishing in cold water, you don't want to use a tropical bonefish line, because those lines are made of materials designed to stay somewhat rigid in intense heat. When you put them in a frigid environment, they remain stiff, and casting a line like that through the guides of a fly rod is tantamount to trying to fire a corkscrew through a straw. Conversely, a coldwater line (like a pike line) withers and turns mushy in hot water—there's no snap in the cast when you want it. So match your line to the conditions, specifically temperatures, you will fish.

Orvis fly line. *Photo courtesy of The Orvis Company*

RIO carp line
Photo by Trevor Tanner

HINT: Too many anglers, in my opinion, credit the rod with 100 percent of casting performance, good or bad, when at least 50 percent of a good cast results from the performance of the fly line itself. Switch lines before you switch rods. Your basic rod can fish anywhere, anytime if you carry some extra lines (and spools for your reel) to match specific water temperatures and the flies you intend to cast.

Finally, anglers like to debate the relevance of color when it comes to fly lines. My short answer to that question is to say a perfect cast makes fly line color irrelevant. Make the right cast, and all the fish sees is the fly, and maybe the leader comes into play a bit. It doesn't matter to me if you "line" a fish with fluorescent orange or mottled gray—you still lined the fish, and the result will, sadly, be the same.

If you're a loop watcher, and having bright orange fly line helps you see how your line behaves in the air or on the water, by all means stick with it. On the other hand, all things being equal, I don't think it can hurt you to cast a camo, tan, gray, or olive fly line.

LEADERS AND TIPPET

Here's where things can get a little tricky, but the "it's up to your personal preferences" rule still applies. I've heard more debate over leaders and tippets than perhaps any other aspect of fly tackle for carp fishing. On the one hand, my Denver friend Will Rice swears by fishing Seaguar 4X fluorocarbon tippet off a RIO 7½-foot, 3X leader—at least when the waters on the South Platte River are running clear. On the other hand, Dave Maynard fishes the same river in all seasons and conditions with 15-pound fluorocarbon. They both catch many fish.

I personally fish a 2X leader chopped back to around 6 feet, then extend the total leader and tippet to around 9 feet by adding 3 feet of 12-pound Maxima. Unless I'm fishing with smaller nymph flies in clear water, in which case I subscribe to the Will Rice program and fish lighter leaders and fluorocarbon tippet, though I usually cannot force myself to go lighter than 3X.

When I'm fishing Lake Michigan, I might go straight to 20-pound Maxima, perhaps tying a short section of Amnesia line from the fly line to the tippet, just to ensure that the larger flies I throw will turn over at the end of a cast, or in a heavy wind.

And when I fish dry flies such as grasshopper imitations to carp, I usually opt for 2X or 3X monofilament tippet tied to a corresponding leader of the same diameter, or one size larger. Remember that fluorocarbon sinks, and monofilament floats, so match the leader and tippet material to the type of fly you use. For example, I don't recommend fishing fluorocarbon with dry flies.

It all comes down to a simple tradeoff. The smaller and more delicate the tippet, the more likely you are to have a carp eat your fly, especially if that's a smaller fly. On the other hand, using light tippet also increases the odds of the fish breaking you off. I tend to think that the size of a tippet factors far less into the equation of whether or not a carp eats a fly than other things like A) the actual fly pattern; B) how well that fly sinks—or doesn't, depending on what you want it to do; and C) the presentation of that fly. In other words, if it looks and acts like real food, the carp is going to eat it, no strings attached, or at least they won't worry about the

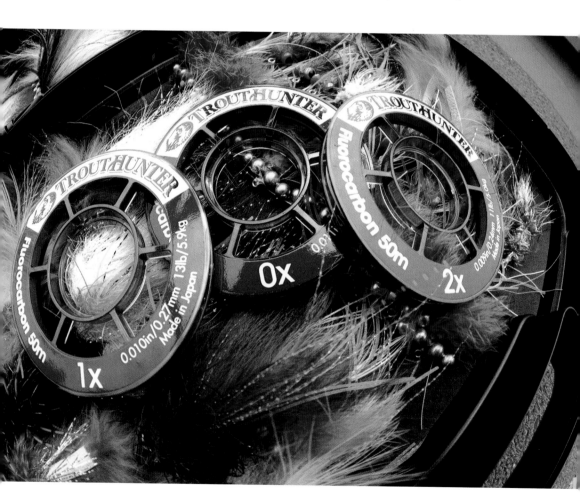

Tippet. *Photo by Cameron Mortenson*

string that really is attached. If the fly looks wrong or acts weird, you can down-size to tippet as scant as a spider's web, and that's not going to save you. But, hav-ing said that, there are times when you need everything going in your favor—the right bug, the right presentation, and a virtually invisible tippet—to earn even a little attention.

The key is knowing when those situations exist, and not assuming that to be the case every time you fish.

HINT: If you master three simple knots, you can successfully catch carp on the fly anywhere in the world. So much is made about knots these days, and they are no doubt important—a subtle difference between one loop knot and leader-to-tippet connection versus another can spell the difference between suc-cess and failure, especially in saltwater. I think of carp fishing as "saltwater fishing" in freshwater environments. But many anglers are intimidated by the knot-tying learning curve. Make it easy on yourself. Learn three knots: A nail knot to tie your fly line to your leader, a double surgeon's knot to connect tippet to the leader, and an improved clinch knot to tie your fly to your tippet. Master those three, and you'll catch plenty of carp, and you can worry about other knots when you want to.

WADERS, BOOTS, NETS, AND OTHER GEAR

When I fly fish for carp, especially in the less-than-pristine environs of an urban river, working around obstacles like shopping carts, rusted cars, and industrial garbage, I wear waders—for obvious reasons. Frankly, in some carp water, wad-ing (especially if you have open sores on your legs) can be a legitimate health concern. I will say that, despite the fact that the water is, in many cases, already crawling with nasty organisms, I still pay attention to wading felt-free, and wash-ing my boots to prevent the spread of invasive species. That sounds like over-kill, but the truth is that for some of these waters to recover, anglers will be the vanguard that makes positive change happen. And clean wading habits matter everywhere.

Left: breathable waders
Below: wading shoes
Photos courtesy of The Orvis Company

As for other ancillary gear for the carp angler, I think a net is usually a good idea. You can try to land carp by hand, but they're typically very slimy and slippery, and by the time you wrestle one into submission and remove the hook barehanded, you cause more harm than you would if you simply scooped it up with a net, pulled the fly, and let the fish go. Carp are not nearly as sensitive as trout when it comes to the slime coating on the skin that protects the fish from diseases, so the net is less a factor. It's still good etiquette to wet your hands before handling any fish, and you want to minimize the "air time" it takes to snap a

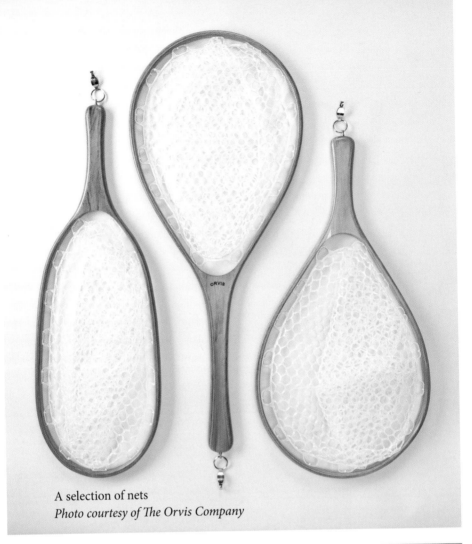

A selection of nets
Photo courtesy of The Orvis Company

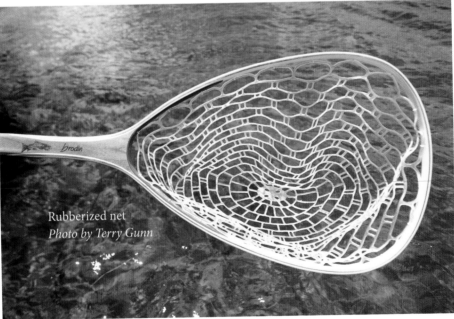

Rubberized net
Photo by Terry Gunn

photograph. As a rule of thumb, hold your own breath as you lift the fish to take a picture—by the time you feel uncomfortable, the fish will as well. But nets make good sense when carp fishing. You might do yourself, and the fish, a favor by using nets with rubberized mesh, as they tend to stick less to the fish and grab flies with less gusto. Go with a model with a large opening/basket, and a long handle.

The only other piece of ancillary gear that I think is critical to carp fishing is a good set of pliers. Carp are able to root into silt several inches deep, and when they find a solid chunk of food, like a snail or a crayfish, they instinctively suck it deep into their mouths, where a set of de facto crusher jaws pulverize the hard shells, well inside their mouths. For this reason, flies are apt to get stuck well inside the carp you catch. A pair of long-nose pliers (you can buy the fancy fishing types with razor-sharp cutters, made of rust-resistant metals, or just a pair from the hardware store will do fine also) can bail the catch-and-release fly angler out of many situations.

Good fishing pliers can be a great help in removing hooks from fish. *Photos courtesy of The Orvis Company*

Photo by Tim Romano

The Approach

15

*T*he number one mistake fly anglers make—and this is true on trout rivers, on bonefish flats, and most certainly in carp-fishing situations—is that they want to impose their will on the fish, rather than letting the fish dictate the agenda. I hate to say it, but no matter how prepared you feel, having read your books and magazine articles, having practiced, and so forth, if you come to the water with a rigid game plan and are unwilling to adapt that plan, you're as good as dead in the water.

The best you can do is to remember some loose guidelines. Regardless of the species of fish a fly angler targets, the whole game can and should always be boiled down to some simple elements: reading the water, in order to find the fish in the first place; picking a fly that looks like something that fish will eat; making a cast (to put that fly in a place where the fish will actually eat it); presenting that fly in a way that makes it behave in a way that the fish will want to eat it; then fighting and subsequently releasing the fish.

We'll base it all on the "Six Fs."

Find the fish.

Then figure out what **Food** they're eating.

Pick the right **Fly**.

Fake the fish out by tricking it with a great presentation.

Fight the fish.

And set the fish **Free**.

Find. Food. Fly. Fake. Fight. Free.

Now, in most situations, from the trout river to the tarpon flats, the angler should consider things in exactly that order, so I will do the same in this

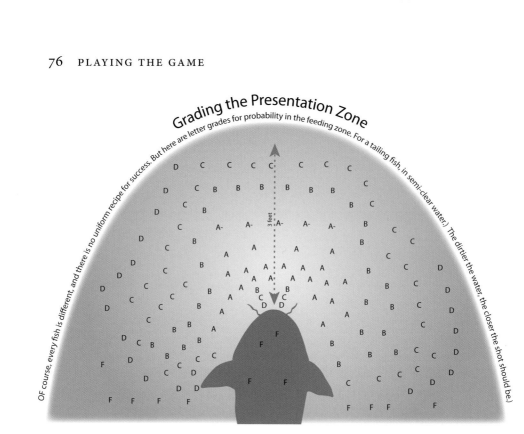

Illustration by Mary Kelley

discussion of carp fishing with flies. Granted, all these factors are always important when it comes to optimal fishing, but if you're going to follow the "crawl,
walk, run" approach when it comes to carp fishing, this should help you focus on
what matters most, in order.

HINT: The best way to get in sync with your fishing environment and let the fish dictate to you how your agenda should
unfold, is simply to stop, wait, and watch the water before you
do anything. Before I even get close to getting my boots wet, I've
made it a habit to sit on the bank and watch the river, lake, or
ocean flat for a good 10 minutes. It doesn't matter if I'm trout
fishing, carp fishing, or tarpon fishing, the time spent surveying
the situation almost always pays dividends. You might see the fish
rising and eating off the surface, and feel inclined to rush to the
water, lest you miss out on an opportunity. I'm telling you, you'll
ruin 100 of those situations for every one you take advantage of
by barreling into the mix. Use your eyes. Have a cup of coffee,
smoke a cigar, whatever. It pays to slow things down and watch.

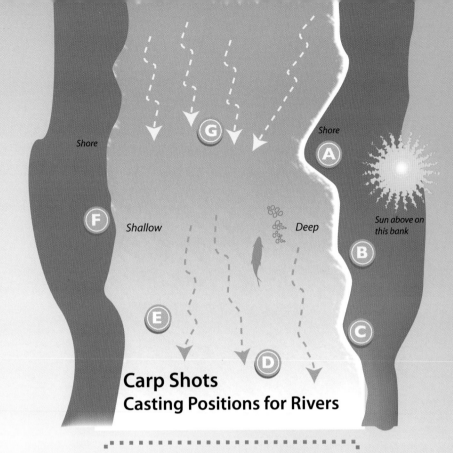

Carp Shots
Casting Positions for Rivers

Carp Shots
Casting Positions for a River

(A) You're in the fish's field of vision. You must be stealthy. Keep a low profile, and cast sparingly. Drift flies or crossing shots.

(B) Not bad, but shadows will be a factor and current will complicate drift/presentation.

(C) A long shot. Short drift. Only a perfect cast works from here.

(D) Don't bother.

(E) Don't bother.

(F) If you can make the long cast and see the fish through the glare, go for it.

(G) You're kidding yourself.

Illustration by Mary Kelley

Photo by Tim Romano

Steve Martinez. *Photo by Kirk Deeter*

Finding Fish: Reading Water and Spotting Carp

16

*W*here do we find carp? Well, as I've told you, carp are typically going to look for warmer water when they want to eat. So, in a lake or a pond, it's important to focus your attention on areas where the wind might be shearing the top layers of the water and forcing them into shallow flats where that water can be cooked by the radiant heat of the sun. Fish the windward side of islands and shorelines, where the water is collected and warmed.

I never had a better lesson in all this than the one taught to me by Steve Martinez and Kevin Morlock as we were fishing the open waters of Lake Michigan around Beaver Island. In confined waters, you have the ability to "divide and conquer" and check out many areas until you actually spot the fish. In huge open waters, like Lake Michigan, the carp can be anywhere. So the carp angler must develop instincts and learn to hone in on the most likely hotspots in order to avoid spending their day on a wild goose chase.

Whether you are fishing in lakes or rivers, there are some fundamental rules that apply to carp, just like any other fish. Number one, fish like changes: changes in currents, changes in structure (rocks, points, and so on), changes in depth, and changes in water temperature. Find the places where the changes are actively happening, and that will help you find the fish.

Second, fish like food. Find the food, and you will find the fish. Typical food sources for carp tend to hang around those "change zones," like structure, weeds, drop-offs, and in the flats where the water warms. With carp, it's often more complex than looking for birds busting on bunker (as an angler might when chasing striped bass, for example), because carp eat so many different things. But if you look toward those change zones, and in bays and stretches of a river where things like insects, fish, and crustaceans might naturally collect, you're well on your way to finding carp.

River carp. *Photo by Brian Bradfield*

Third, fish want a "Plan B." In other words, they seldom venture into places where there isn't an escape route readily at hand. Of course, it's a different story in confined areas like golf course ponds, but by and large, even in those situations, carp will gravitate to areas where they aren't far away from the cover of weeds, or near a ledge where they can plunge into deep water. On a river, you'll find that carp will occasionally get into wide, shallow flats, but the highest concentrations of fish are going to stick fairly close to the deep pools, or the bends in the river where the willows hang over the surface, or where the vegetation grows thick.

If you think of those three things, paying extra careful attention to other aspects like currents (that flush food), and wind (that collects food, and helps to warm certain areas of water), you've licked 90 percent of the challenge of finding carp, no matter if you're fishing a huge lake, a river, or a small pond.

HINT: DON'T STOP AT THE FIRST FISH YOU FIND.

There's a difference between finding a carp, and finding a carp that's a "player." When we're diligently walking up a riverbank, looking for fish, natural instinct tells us to stop and cast at the first fish we see. That can be a mistake, especially when carp fishing.

For example, say you're walking up a river, and you notice a big carp cruising along a point. Your mind might tell you to fire away at that fish, but it may be a better idea, in fact, to retreat from the bank, and walk downstream a bit to see what's happening in the calmer flat below. Many times I have felt inclined to fish to the first carp I saw, but I was either talked into walking on or simply felt a hunch. And downstream, in that calmer flat water, I found dozens of carp eagerly tailing and eating. Had I fired a cast at the first fish, might I have spooked the others? With carp, that's entirely possible. It's always best to survey as much of the landscape as you can before committing to the cast. Carp fishing might be one of those few cases where a "bird in hand" might not, in fact, be better than those in the nearby bush.

SPOTTING FISH

Let's face it, the real appeal of carp fishing is sight casting. Being able to see the fish you target before you make a cast is top of the game. It's what fuels the addiction for many fly anglers. That's why people fly halfway around the world to sight-cast in the gin-clear trout rivers of New Zealand; it's why anglers will bake for hours under the subtropical sun of Florida's Ten Thousand Islands hoping for a shot at a "laid-up" tarpon, and it's why I fly fish for carp in the first place. Put it this way: If catching carp were all about using sinking lines to swing streamers steelhead style, or drifting nymphs under a strike indicator at invisible fish, then fly fishing for carp wouldn't interest me in the least. It all about stalking and spotting.

To that end, I think carp offer amazing sight-fishing opportunities in the unlikeliest of places. I'm on record for saying that I think some of the best sight-fishing flats in America can be found off Beaver Island in Lake Michigan—as well as in the Florida Keys and in the Hawaiian Islands. In fact, I call Michigan the "Carpatan Peninsula," and Beaver Island is "Beaver Key."

Costas polarized sunglasses. *Photo by Cameron Mortenson*

Before you laugh and fly thousands of miles to Mexico's Yucatan Peninsula to catch bonefish and permit (which is, no doubt, absolutely wonderful), consider that on the right day in certain parts of the Great Lakes, a wading angler can stalk, spot, cast to, hook, and land hundreds of pounds of fish in classic flats style. You just have to accept the fact that those fish are carp.

And, of course, you have to be able to see them.

Spotting carp starts with good polarized sunglasses. Polarized eyewear is available in many lens tints, and every angler has his or her own preferences. Most of the serious carp anglers I know like to fish with amber or copper lenses. On particularly bright days, grays and mirrored blue or mirrored green lenses work well. And in low-light conditions, yellow lenses might offer the best contrast. The types of frames you choose, and how much you spend, are purely matters of individual choice. But polarized glasses are as important a gear consideration when fly fishing for carp as your rod, reel, and the flies you use. If you don't have any, it's pretty hard to do.

This next tip will sound like a Yogi Berra-ism, but the secret to spotting fish is knowing where to look. That's true with any type of sight fishing, from the trout river to the bonefish flats. As I just explained, the more you are able to focus your gaze in areas where fish are most likely to be, the more likely you are to see them.

Then it becomes a matter of understanding and identifying subtle indicators. Very rarely will you see a whole fish, all at once. It's the tip of a tail, a slight wake,

Tailing carp. *Photo by Mark Erdosy*

perhaps the metallic glint of scales reflecting in the sunlight, and noticing inconsistent patterns of shadows and colors while looking through the water column that gives the fish away.

HINT: "THROUGH THE SCREEN DOOR"

When I spot fish, the first thing I do is create a mental template, and focus my gaze inside that template. I create an imaginary viewing pane, about the size of a house door. I turn that door sideways in my mind, and then place that viewing pane over patches of water where I think I might see fish. Looking through the "glass" of that imaginary door, I study everything within the perimeter of my template, starting with the surface. Are there any ripples? Wakes? Fins? I then look through the water column (don't just look at the water, look through it). Any shadows or inconsistent colors? Any motion? Lastly I'll fix my stare right on the bottom, again looking for inconsistent colors that don't match the sand or gravel of the bottom, flashes, shadows, or motion.

It's a process of elimination. After I've spent plenty of time (which might be a minute or more looking through that single door-size template) and I don't see fish, I'll "lift and place" that template on another area, follow the same steps, and repeat that process over and over until I either see a fish, or conclude that none are there—which, of course, doesn't always mean that there really are no fish there).

The key thing to remember is that you can't find fish by looking for a whole fish in an entire body of water. You must divide and conquer, looking piece by piece, for pieces of fish.

There are other telltales that give carp away, especially in shallow or "skinny" water. A bonefish guide will tell an angler to look for "nervous water," or areas of the surface that are inconsistent with their surroundings. You'll also learn to use nervous water as a signal for carp, and nervous water can indicate a school of fish, or even the individual cruiser. Sometimes you'll note slight ripples, even wakes, pushing and moving along.

Part of spotting fish is learning to eliminate what's not a reliable telltale—wind ripples, sticks and deadfall, currents sweeping around rocks, and other factors can often trick you into thinking a fish is somewhere it isn't. All I can say in that regard is to check out everything that looks suspicious, and spend the time to see if it moves. With time and experience, you'll hone your instincts to better tell you what's really a fish and what isn't.

MUDS

Plumes of silt on the bottom of a slow-moving river or in a lake will also indicate where carp are eating. As they root around for food, they kick up a trail behind them, so casting toward the front edge of a well-defined and moving mud cloud is often worth the shot, even if you can't make out the fish clearly.

Unfortunately, the sudden appearance of a mud cloud in close proximity to where you wade more often than not tells you that you've just spooked a fish (or several), and they're no longer players.

Mudding carp. *Photo by Kevin Morlock*

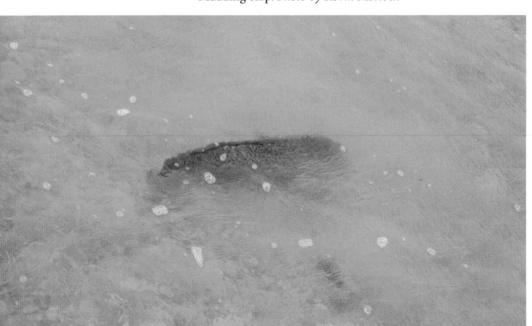

Looking for tailing carp. *Photo by Will Rice*

TAILS AND FINS

Spotting tailing fish is the carp angler's nirvana—not only will the tip of a tail glimmering in the sunlight tell you exactly where the fish is, it also tells you that the fish is eating, tilting its mouth to the bottom as it vacuums in food. Tailing carp are happy carp, and usually the easiest to catch. You might also see a carp roll, revealing its dorsal fin and back, which also gives you a clear indication of where the fish is pointed and moving, though a roller is less happy and less likely to eat, usually, than a tailer.

There are three tricks to remember when looking for tailing carp. Foremost, the angler wants to be acutely aware of the sun's position overhead. It's far easier to see subtle shapes and contrasts when the sun is behind you. Staring straight into the glare is a nonstarter that makes spotting tails difficult. Put your body in the right position before you start looking for fish. That said, understand that with the sun at your back, you will also create shadows, so be mindful about where those shadows are cast, relative to the water you're scanning.

LIPS

Of course, you can spot carp by watching them suck food (like berries, seeds, or insects) off the water's surface. Sometimes that appears as a sudden, slight dimple in the water, and sometimes it's a more pronounced roll and slurp.

Photo by Kirk Deeter

One of the oddest things I've ever seen while fly fishing for carp happened on Lake Henshaw in southern California, when cattle grazing in the hayfields by the lake kicked up swarms of grasshoppers, which flew through the air, were swept by the prevailing breeze out over the lake, and fell into the choppy water. (See page 49.) From the carp's perspective, it was literally gobs of protein falling from the sky, and the fish had an uncanny ability to recognize this almost as soon as it happened.

I was fishing with Conway Bowman and John Hendrickson (two of San Diego's most decorated saltwater guides, known for chasing mako sharks with flies), when we noticed the carp grouped up in bunches, their lips pressed in circles just above the surface, no doubt waiting for the unfortunate grasshoppers to float into range. The mouths of these carp looked like bowls of uncooked calamari rings, and they appeared in sporadic pods throughout the lake, usually right on the white foam current lines formed by the wind. If we dropped a grasshopper fly in the bowl of calamari, it often got bit. But many times, as soon as the lips would appear, they'd vanish under the surface.

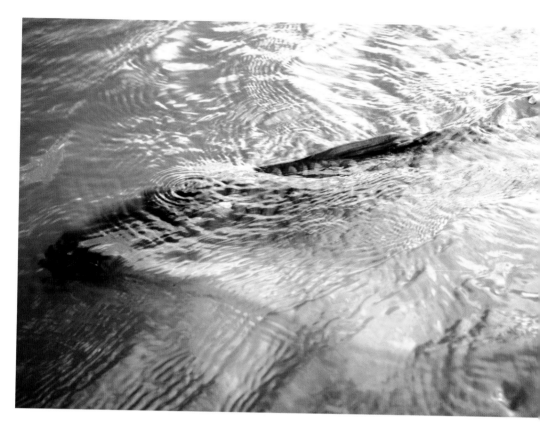

Photo by Kirk Deeter

FIND OUT MORE ABOUT BOWMAN BLUEWATER

Which leads me to my last point about spotting carp. When you are able to see a fish—be that a tail poking above the surface, or a shadow lurking along the bottom—do you best to maintain fairly steady eye contact. Naturally, your mind will shift to other tasks at hand, like getting your fly ready, making the cast, and so forth, but maintaining eye contact as much as possible will help you set up for a cast that matters.

Photo by Kevin Morlock

Figuring Out Food

17

*I*n carp fishing, fly anglers learn to separate the "players" from the "contenders." By reading their body positions—the way the carp move or suspend in the water—you'll be able to understand which fish offer you a decent opportunity, and which do not. You'll also be able to form hunches about what those carp are eating. Reading the fish themselves will often tell you what foods they prefer.

To this end, I separate carp into five categories: "top feeders" (those you can literally watch sipping food off the surface of a river or a lake); "suspended fish," which hover above the bottom, yet below the surface, and stay in place; "current riders," which stay in one place (usually in a river) and wait for the food to float to them; "cruisers," which move along the bottom in a predictable pattern, vacuuming food into their mouths as they swim; and "tailers," which, like bonefish, tip their snouts into the muck, showing their tails as they tilt their bodies. Recognizing the "stages" of feeding carp is key to success, as each situation will suggest to an angler how best to present a fly. Let's look at each scenario on a case-by-case basis.

TOP FEEDERS

Encountering top-feeding carp may well be the best-case scenario. There's not a lot of mystery involved. If you can actually see what they're eating, and put a fly that represents that particular food source in the target zone, you'll get bit, more often than not. Of course, the "figuring out what they're eating" part is easier said than done.

Step one is to slow down, take a rest, sit on the bank of the lake or river, and simply watch. Observing and absorbing what's really going on is more important when it comes to carp fishing than it is in any other fly-fishing scenario.

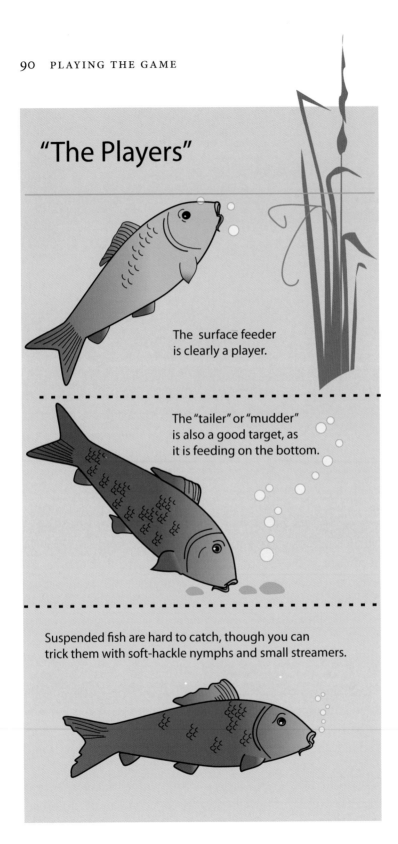

"The Players"

The surface feeder is clearly a player.

The "tailer" or "mudder" is also a good target, as it is feeding on the bottom.

Suspended fish are hard to catch, though you can trick them with soft-hackle nymphs and small streamers.

Illustration by Mary Kelley

Maybe the fish are eating grasshoppers. Do you see naturals on the water? Maybe they're parked under a tree that's dropping berries. What are the telltales that might indicate to you the type of fly you should tie on? When you're confident about the fly pattern you should throw (and not before!) find a place to make that cast, and float your fly in a way that perfectly mimics the natural food source the carp are keyed into.

SUSPENDED FISH

They look like torpedoes, silhouettes under the water's surface, but as you watch them, you realize they aren't moving much at all.

These are the hardest carp to catch. I've made literally thousands of casts at suspended carp over the past several years, and I've hooked few of those fish. My best shot happened just off Beaver Island in Lake Michigan, where I saw a suspended carp in about 10 feet of clear water as I fished from a boat. I made a "what the heck" roll cast and dropped a minnow pattern inches from the fish's face. It took one look, then gulped it down. The only reason that cast and that fly worked is because the fish wasn't wise to the presence of the boat (the cast was in front of the boat). And I was really lucky. I triggered an impulse eat. But I have made many similar casts, with no effect, before and after that lucky shot (it was a 20-pound fish), and I'd say that catching a suspended carp is a total crapshoot. They're worth trying, but keep your expectations low. Otherwise, you'll drive yourself insane.

CURRENT RIDERS

In river environments, carp will sometimes stake out a spot in a juicy current and wait for the food to flow down to them, no differently than a trout or a bass. In these situations, the angler simply has to play the trout game: Make an upstream cast, let your flies sink, and hit the carp in the face. They're either going to eat it or not. If you're lucky enough to make multiple casts without spooking the fish, be sure to switch fly patterns. If you know the fish saw what you had to offer but didn't eat it, take a break, and tie on a different pattern. You're not going to beat the fish into submission by drifting the same bug, over and over. Pause, tie on something else, and give that a ride. If you're refused again, follow the same plan for as long as you can before you spook the fish.

CRUISERS

A carp that's diligently, methodically working a path along the bottom of the river or lake is, no doubt, a player, despite what you may have heard otherwise. Your best chance for hooking a carp on a fly in big open water, like the Great Lakes, is by tricking a cruiser. In this situation it's all about two things: making a cast that puts the fly in the immediate frontal vicinity of that cruising carp, and having that fly sink fast enough (or slowly enough) to be suspended at exactly the right level (or touching the bottom) at the precise moment when the carp swims into the feeding zone.

I am fully convinced that, if you put any fly at the right depth and proximity in front of cruising carp, more often than not they're going to eat the fly. This might in fact be the one scenario when the angler has the advantage. Put it right there, make the carp see it, give it the appropriate action, and you have as good a chance as any to have the fish eat that fly. Doesn't matter if it's a nymph, a streamer, or some weird fly pattern—if they're cruising and eating along the way, and you serve your fly up on the platter, they're likely going to eat it.

TAILERS

As just mentioned, this is the "carp nirvana" scenario, when you see fish tailing in skinny water. You know where they are, especially when their golden tails glisten in the sunlight. Sometimes, you can key on tailers by watching for mud clouds in deeper water. When you see a line of muddy water moving from right to left, for example, you know that there are multiple fish rooting around and eating on the bottom. In either situation it's important to lead the fish, but not too much. You want to drop your fly right into the production line. Pop, pop, pop, and (when it's your turn), bang. Set the hook.

I always like to be on the upcurrent side of the feeding progression when it comes to fishing for tailers. Your odds go down incrementally when you try to catch up to the fish, essentially casting from where they were to where they're going to be. Best to position yourself on the "where they're going to be" side of the feeding pattern with a downcurrent cast, and let them swim into your fly.

So let's bring this all together. When you see carp feeding off the water's surface, you know they're eating insects such as mayflies, grasshoppers, beetles, ants, and so forth, or they're eating something like seeds or berries that have fallen into the river. (Okay, maybe they're eating corn chips or cigarette butts.) But even a little time surveying the waterscape should lock you right in on the correct fly pattern. If you're in the middle of a lake, fishing from a boat, for example, it's pretty doubtful that the carp are sucking down mulberries, so I'd be thinking about mayflies and grasshoppers and looking carefully at the bugs to match accordingly.

When you see carp suspended in the water, you know you're in a tough situation. But in those cases, it's often worth tossing a small mayfly nymph or a worm pattern in close proximity to the fish. In open water, it might be worth showing them a streamer that looks like a baitfish.

And when you see carp tailing, rooting around on the bottom, that's when you know it's time to throw a crayfish, or a small weighted nymph, or even something that looks like a freshwater clam.

HINT: PRIORITIZE YOUR CARP

All things being equal, I'll always trade up, from a shot at a cruiser to a shot at a tailer, or a shot at a rising carp. And when I see tailing carp, I start small with my flies, and build up in size if I'm not getting noticed. In trout fishing, the mantra is to make a presentation, and if you get refused, size down. In carp fishing, start small, and if you don't get noticed, only then do you size up.

Photo by Kirk Deeter

Picking the Right Fly

18

*T*his is another area of hot debate among fly-fishing-for-carp enthusiasts. One school of thought holds that carp have such keen senses, and that you're only trying to trick one of them (vision), that too much focus on the exact fly pattern is wasted effort. Put the fly where the carp can see it and react to it, and if you do that well, they just might eat it. Do it wrong, and even if you have the "Mother of All Carp Flies" on the end of your tippet, it's not going to matter.

The other school of thought is that because carp can notice colors and are tuned into things like the profile of a fly, it pays dividends to find that perfect fly pattern that not only looks the part, but also acts the part, meaning you can work it so it lands quietly, swims naturally, and has alluring (if not irresistible) action.

I firmly believe that some flies are designed to catch fish, and other flies are designed to catch fly fishers. As such, staple, time-tested patterns like Whit's Hoppers, Parachute Adams, Pheasant Tail Nymphs, and Woolly Buggers are always in my fly box—and yes, I mean my carp fly box, too. But I'm also constantly checking out the new colors, materials, and profiles that might give me an edge (at least a mental edge). I do think that some of the newer materials—the foams, flashy synthetics, tungsten weights, and so forth—can make fly patterns more effective, especially for carp.

I also believe in being different. If you're fishing a lake where your buddy sent you, and he told you that he fishes a rust Woolly Bugger and just tears 'em up, and you know he fishes there often, why in the heck would you throw the exact same pattern? Sure, there's something to be said for proven performance, but I like to be just a tad different and show the carp something they might not have seen before. In that case, I might throw an Autumn Splendor streamer. On the hopper lake where everyone's using a Schroeder's Hopper, I'll throw a Michigan Skunk, especially in Colorado or Idaho—that really tricks the fish and my friends. If the report says the hot bug is a Beadhead Pheasant Tail, I'll throw a soft-hackle Pheasant Tail. Familiarity breeds contempt when it comes to carp, and marching to the beat of your own drummer, perhaps wandering off the beaten path just a little bit, often pays huge dividends when it comes to fly fishing for carp. Of course, the more you experiment and devise your own carp fly patterns at your fly tying bench, the better.

With that preamble out of the way, I'm going to offer up a list of 21 carp fly staple patterns that are always in my box. You'll notice that they're not all purely "carp flies," by design, rather flies that I know will catch carp.

Backstabber. *All Photos by Kirk Deeter*

BACKSTABBER, #6, rusty (Zimmerman)

This is a great all-around crayfish pattern that can be twitched along the bottom of a lake or pond, or even dead-drifted toward carp feeding in a river. The trick is to put this fly in plain sight, but make it "escape" as you retrieve it.

HOOK: Gamakatsu SL45, #6.

THREAD: UNI-Thread 6/0, tan.

EYES: Spirit River Dazl-Eyes, 1/8, gold.

BODY: Dave Whitlock SLF Dubbing (red fox squirrel nymph abdomen).

TOP: Marabou blood quills (burnt orange).

TACKLE: Brown Brahma hen soft-hackle.

Hammerhead

HAMMERHEAD, 2/0, olive (Anderson)

The beauty of this fly is that it sinks fast, right into the zone. It's especially deadly where big carp are cruising shallow, clear flats, but it also works well in dirty water. This is a Beaver Island staple.

HOOK: Mustad R74, #4.

THREAD: 3/0 or size A mono or Flymaster Plus, color to match body.

EYES: X-large gold bead chain and 8–10 wraps of .030 lead wire.

TAIL: 4–6 pumpkin/black flake Sili Legs, 6 strands glow-in-the-dark Mylar Motion fluorescent orange, 6 strands glow-in-the-dark Mylar Motion fluorescent yellow.

UNDERBODY: Dark brown sparkle yarn.

OVERBODY: Crayfish orange Magnum Zonker or black-barred orange over tan Hareline tiger-barred Magnum.

Meat Whistle

MEAT WHISTLE, #1/0, crawdad (Barr)

I prefer this fly for carp over any other streamer pattern. The offset hook eye helps the fly undulate and adds appealing action as you strip it slowly, gently along the bottom.

HOOK: Gamakatsu 90-degree jig hook, #1/0.
CONE: Large tungsten cone, copper.
THREAD: UTC 140-denier, rusty brown.
RIBBING: Brassie-sized UTC Ultra Wire, copper brown.
BODY: Sparkle Braid, copper.
WING: Rabbit strip, rusty brown.
LEGS: Sili Legs, pumpkin barred.
FLASH: Copper Flashabou.
COLLAR: Brown marabou.

GREAT LAKES GOBY, #3/0, tan (Cushman)

In those rare instances where you find carp keyed almost exclusively on baitfish (as in certain regions of the Great Lakes), this pattern is a staple. Be sure to give it some action, though. Make it swim and stall; the more wounded it appears, the greater the odds of earning a bite.

HOOK: Gamakatsu Jig, 90-degree.
THREAD: Danville beige, 140-denier.
TAIL: Fuzzy Fiber, tan and golden brown, blended; Softex at the base of tail.
BODY: Fuzzy Fiber, tan and golden brown, blended; Softex to make pectoral fins.
EYES: Lead dumbbell, painted yellow.

Great Lakes Goby

DEAD DRIFT CRAYFISH, #8, olive (Haddon)

Yes, the name implies river fishing where the current is steady, but this is also a very effective lake pattern, especially in clear water where the carp are extremely selective and tend to scrutinize every fly.

HOOK: Tiemco 5263, #8.
THREAD: Danville 6/0, black.
EYES: Small bead chain.
WEIGHT: Lead wire, .025.
ANTENNAE: Rabbit fur and turkey tail, crayfish orange.
FLASH: Root Beer Krystal Flash.
CLAW: Rabbit strips, black-barred crayfish orange.
SHELLBACK: Mottled Thin Skin.
RIB: Black wire, medium.
BODY: Blend of burnt orange and olive dubbing.
HACKLE: Saddle hackle, ginger.

Dead Drift Crayfish

GEEZUS LIZARD, #1/0, crayfish (Zimmerman)

Yet another crayfish pattern, this well-weighted gaudy bug drops like a rock, so it's great for "smart bombing" river pockets and areas where you need to make a pattern show up quickly. It doubles as a great bass pattern.

HOOK: Gamakatsu Jig 90, heavy-wire (round bend) #2 and #1/0.

THREAD: Tail, Danville's 210 Flymaster Plus (black); body, Danville's 3/0 waxed monocord.

TIP: Frog's Hair dubbing (golden yellow), Dub 1: Whitlock SLF (dark stone nymph), Dub 2: Whitlock SLF NearNuff Crayfish natural orange).

LEGS: Spirit River Tarantu-legs hot orange, medium.

BELLY: Hareline Dubbin Scud Back ¼" clear.

RIB: UTC Ultra Wire, black, medium.

BODY: Rear: dark rust Micro Mink on #2, rabbit on #1/0; front: lite rust Micro Mink on #2, rabbit on #1/0.

TOP: Dark brown marabou.

EYES: Yellow dumbbells, medium on #2, large on #1/0.

HEAD: Whitlock SLF Dark Dragonfly.

Geezus Lizard. *All Photos by Kirk Deeter*

BC HOPPER-DROPPER, #8 (Barr/Craven)

One of the best all-around hopper patterns for any type of fly fishing, carp and trout included. The BC Hopper is hard to sink, so it matches well with the morsel nymph pattern you might choose to trail behind it.

HOOK: TMC 5262, #4–10.

THREAD: 3/0 monocord, tan.

BODY: 3mm foam, tan.

BINDER STRIP: Scrap of 3mm foam.

ADHESIVE: Zap-A-Gap.

HOPPER LEGS: Round rubber leg, tan.

UNDERWING: Mottled tan Web Wing.

FLASH: Root Beer Krystal Flash.

OVERWING: Elk hair.

BULLET HEAD: Natural deer hair.

FRONT LEGS: Round rubber legs, tan.

INDICATOR: McFlylon or Float Viz.

BC Hopper-Dropper.

Epoxy Mantis Shrimp

EPOXY MANTIS SHRIMP, #6, brown (Bachmann)
HOOK: Tiemco 800s.
THREAD: Danville Brown 6/0.
TAIL: Tan marabou.
BODY: Estaz Petite Root Beer.
EYES: Melted monofilament, colored with black marker.
HACKLE: Barred ginger rooster.
CLAW: Grizzly variant Indian rooster, Accent Flash Pearl.
HEAD: Gold bead chain medium, hot glue, brown marker.
LEGS: Sili Legs, pumpkin/black flake.
WEEDGUARD: 30 lb. hard mono.
Who says you can't use saltwater flies for carp? Not me! I use them all the time. Granted, you don't find natural shrimp floating around in Midwestern lakes and rivers, but the bugginess and action of this pattern make it a money attractor.

Clouser Minnow

CLOUSER MINNOW, #8, various colors (Clouser)
Bob Clouser's pattern is easy to tie, and so darned effective that any serious carp angler (or trout angler, or saltwater angler, or bass angler) would be remiss not to have plenty in the arsenal. I gravitate toward that stark black-and-white contrast when I'm fishing for carp, particularly in stained water.
HOOK: TMC 811S, #2/0, #2, and #6, weighted.
THREAD: Black 6/0.
EYES: Lead hourglass eyes, painted dark red with black pupils.
TAIL: Black bucktail.
BODY: Black bucktail (top)/white bucktail (bottom).
WING: Black bucktail with dark green Krystal Flash.

San Juan Worm

SAN JUAN WORM, #10, various colors
Most of us "fly fishers" go to great lengths to distance ourselves from being "worm dunkers," yet being honest about how many different fish we catch on worm patterns would send us straight to the confessional. Get real—all fish love to eat worms, and carp are foremost in the mix. I like patterns that undulate in the current. Red is a staple, but don't forget about brown and tan also.
HOOK: TMC 2457, #6–10.
THREAD: Red 6/0.

ABDOMEN: Red vernille or ultra chenille, singed with a flame at both ends.
BEAD: Copper, size to fit hook.

Rubber-Legged Hare's-ear
All Photos by Kirk Deeter

RUBBER-LEGGED HARE'S-EAR, #12, gray

Carp certainly love to eat nymph flies, but there's something special about rubber legs in a pattern that helps to trick the bite. Fish this one different ways—dead-drift it in river currents, but don't be afraid to lay it down and start some subtle twitches in flatwater environs.

HOOK: #10–14.
THREAD: Black or brown.
BEAD: (optional): Tungsten (optional).
TAIL: Hare's-ear.
BODY: Hare's-ear dubbing.
RIB: Round tinsel, gold.
LEGS: Rubber legs, black and white.
THORAX: Hare's-ear dubbing.
WINGCASE: Pheasant fibers.

Copper John

COPPER JOHN (RUBBER LEGS) #10, black (Barr)

See the last entry for rationale about rubber legs, but John Barr's ingenuity made this pattern sink faster than most hairy bugs. This is my go-to dropper pattern when I'm fishing the dry-dropper combo for carp.

HOOK: Tiemco 2487, #10.
THREAD: 210-denier flat waxed, black.
BEAD: River Spirits gold.
BODY: UTC Ultra Wire, medium.
TAIL: Goose biots.
THORAX: Peacock swords.
LEGS: Small round rubber, black.
FLASH: Flashabou.
THORAX: Epoxy.

Darth Clam. *Photo by Lipton*

DARTH CLAM (Lipton)

In some places, for instance in the Columbia River between Washington and Oregon, carp will root around and find clams as their favored protein source. You just have to put this one in the right place at the right time, and wait for the pickup.

HOOK: Mustad 34007/S71SZ, #6 or 8.
THREAD: UNI-thread 6/0, brown.
BEAD: 6mm, gunmetal.
BODY: Furry Foam, brown.
TAG: Ultra Chenille, pink.

Tabou Daddy. *Photo by Schweitzer*

TABOU DADDY (Schweitzer)

This might be the most realistic crayfish pattern of all. You can fish this one in a variety of ways, from the drop and stop, to the slow, deliberate twitch along a sandy bottom.

HOOK: 3X streamer hook. A #12 is used in this example.
THREAD: 8/0.
WEIGHT: Lead wire.
HEAD: Hareline Dubbin Ice Dub, rusty brown.
PINCERS: A grizzly-dyed brown rooster soft hackle with chickabou pelt.
LEGS: Grizzly-dyed brown rooster soft-hackle, Woolly Bugger style.
EYES: 0.012" monofilament.
BODY: Hareline Dubbin Ice Dub, rusty brown.

Soft-hackle Pheasant Tail

SOFT-HACKLE PHEASANT TAIL

Soft-hackle nymphs are especially useful for carp—the oscillating action of the hackle often triggers at least some investigation. The beadhead variety will naturally sink faster, and can be fished near the bottom. Use soft-hackles without beads when you are targeting suspended fish, especially in river pools. In either case, when you fish a soft-hackle, you want to really slow down your retrieve, making twitches rather than long strips, in order to accentuate the action of the fly.

HOOK: MFC1XL 7076, bronze #6 to 12.
THREAD: UNI-Thread, rusty brown.
BEAD: MFC brass bead, black (optional).
BODY: Natural pheasant tail and Wing N'Flash, lime.
HACKLE: Hungarian partridge, natural.
RIB: Copper wire.

Warmwater Prince
All Photos by Kirk Deeter

WARMWATER PRINCE, #6

Is it a streamer, or is it a nymph? In the carp context, it's actually both. This is an especially hot pattern on more pressured river carp environments, such as Denver's South Platte River. You can turn over a million rocks and not find any "natural" bug that looks anything like it, but that combo of peacock herl in the body and the undulating tail makes it a deadly choice for finicky fish, especially when you strip it ever so slowly through the strike zone.

HOOK: TFC 5444 60 Jig, #2–6.
THREAD: 6/0 olive.
BEAD: Gold, to match hook size.
WEIGHT: Lead substitute, to suit sink rate desired.
TAIL: Brown marabou with root beer highlights.
RIB: Holographic tinsel, olive, medium.
BODY: Peacock herl twisted around olive UNI-Wire, extra-small.
HACKLE: Brown hen back or brown grizzly, 3–4 turns.
LEGS: Olive Centipede, medium.
WING: White goose biot.
COLLAR: Arizona Dubbing, natural.

Crazy Charley

CRAZY CHARLEY, #8, tan

You can't get any more old-school in a bonefish context than the Crazy Charley. It's a staple for fish rooting around in the sand for food, and the same is true when you chase carp. If you see a tailer, try a Charley. Put it no more than 2 feet away from its snout, let it settle, give it a pronounced pop or two, and see what happens.

HOOK: TMC 811S, #4–8.
THREAD: 3/0, tan.
EYES: Chrome bead chain.
BODY: Clear V-rib over pearl Flashabou.
WING: Tan calf tail.

Parachute Adams

PARACHUTE ADAMS, #10, gray

If the situation even hints of mayflies, and carp are eating on the surface, you need one pattern in the box, and this is it. Drop it in the rings left on the surface by a feeding fish and wait. But if the fish doesn't eat, don't rip it off the surface. Nudge it out of the zone, wait a good minute or so, and go again.

HOOK: TMC 100, sizes #12–22.
THREAD: Gray, 6/0.
WING: White calf tail.
TAIL: Grizzly hackle fibers.

BODY: Gray muskrat.
HACKLE: Brown grizzly.

ALL-PURPOSE NYMPH, #12, black (Puyans)

"All-purpose" pretty much says it all. Rivers, lakes, ponds . . . if the carp are eating nymphs, this pattern is money. But you have to make it swim, ever so slightly, inch by inch.
HOOK: TMC 3761, #10–18, weighted.
THREAD: Black 6/0.
TAIL: Dark moose.
ABDOMEN: Black beaver or Hare-Tron.
RIB: Copper wire.
WINGCASE: Dark moose.
The list could go on forever, as well it should. Don't limit yourself. Try different patterns, invent your own, and fish them in different ways. The most valuable fly in the carp angler's fly box is one that can be fished 100 different ways.

All-Purpose Nymph

CARP BITTERS, #6, mango (Reynolds)

Alternative colors for the Carp Bitters are olive and rust.
HOOK: Gamakatsu SL45.
THREAD: Ultra Thread burnt orange, 140-denier.
TAIL: Grizzly marabou, dyed orange.
UNDERBODY: Lead wire, .020.
BODY: Craw Dub, softshell.
EYES: Bead chain, black, medium.
LEGS: Sili Legs, barred orange.
COLLAR: Indian hen, dyed orange.

Carp Bitters

MARABOU PUFF FLY (Klewein)

HOOK: Nymph hook, wide gap, short shank, #10–12.
THREAD: 6/0 olive or black.
BODY: Variegated marabou, olive, brown, or purple.
RIB: Copper wire.
THORAX: Palmered peacock herl.

Marabou Puff Fly

Photo by Erin Block

Photo by Kevin Morlock

Fooling Carp: The Cast and Presentation

19

THE CARP CAST

In the trout-fishing world, the cast is not nearly as important as other factors, including your fly selection and your presentation. (With dry flies and nymphs, that's usually a natural dead-drift.) In saltwater fly fishing, the cast is paramount. If you can't put that fly in a place where the target fish can see it in the first place, the game is over before it starts.

Carp fishing is like saltwater fishing in this regard. A good, accurate, and often long cast is always important. As stated previously, the perfect carp cast lands the fly mere inches to maybe a foot or so directly in front of the target fish.

But alas, that perfect carp cast doesn't necessarily require unfurling 80 feet of fly line. Sometimes it does, but I've seen plenty of casts catch carp within a range of 20 feet, especially in murky water.

Carp are notoriously spooky fish, as explained earlier, and sounds and vibrations will ruin many opportunities. But if you are stealthy enough to wade into position and make a short, accurate cast, you'll up your odds of hooking a fish exponentially.

When it comes to casting at carp, accuracy always trumps distance.

PERCENTAGES

Most fishing guides will tell you that your odds of hooking up on a targeted fish diminish incrementally with every cast. With trout, your chances decrease maybe 10 percent with every cast you make. With a cruising bonefish, that might be 20 percent.

In terms of carp, I'd say that your chances go down 50 percent with each and every cast. In other words, when you cast once and it doesn't work, you can try again, but that second cast is a 50–50 proposition. You might take another cast, but at that point, at best, it's a 1-in-100 prospect. It happens, but it's a longshot.

What's the lesson? You must make your first cast at a carp count. Period.

Before I cast at any carp, I take extra time to factor in things like wind and distance. To gauge distance, I false cast away from my target, and only when I feel confident do I unfurl that shot where I intend for it to sail.

False casts ruin opportunities. And even though carp are smellers and listeners, remember that they're lookers, too. You shouldn't assume they cannot sense the danger from an overhead predator. Watch a blue heron fly over a carp-strewn flat, see the fish scatter, and you'll know what I mean.

So all the fancy loops, and all the *A River Runs Through It* shadow casts, don't amount to a hill of beans on the carp flat. In fact, false casts flat out ruin opportunities. With every false cast over a target carp, I'd say your chances of actually hooking that fish diminish by 50 percent as well.

So don't make false casts, ever, at least not over or in the general direction of a targeted carp. Cast to the side until you can gauge the right distance, and then let the money cast fly. Or better yet, learn to use the surface of the water to load the rod. The water load is done by stripping in all your slack line to create a tight connection with the fly line that is still on the water. Keep your rod tip pointed low. When your rod tip is high, you have no leverage to accelerate the rod, which defeats the purpose. With the rod tip low, lift the rod forcefully, but not loudly, to allow the water's surface to create resistance, which puts flex into the rod. This is known as "loading the rod." Stop the rod abruptly on the backcast to generate more line speed, and shoot the extra line out the back to garner the length you want to achieve. Then stop the line again ("hauling" the line with your noncasting hand grabbing the line) and redirect that cast directly toward the target. Let it fly, and drop it. If you practice this, you should be able to simply lift . . . stop (with a haul) . . . redirect . . . and shoot the line on your target in one graceful motion. It isn't about power or strength; it's all about timing and tempo. But if you learn to water load your line, you should be able to cast accurately 50 feet or more with a simple three-step move: lift, stop, and fire.

The water load is the key to the carp cast. You can dabble with roll casts, reach casts, and all those things, but for me, when it comes to carp, it's all about up and down, lift and place, once and done.

That's because sound is the primary inhibiting factor when it comes to casting at carp. Make loud clatter on an aluminum boat as you drift into casting range, and you're as good as finished. Grind your boots on the gravel of a river bottom as you approach a tailing carp, and that spells game over as well.

That said, 90 percent of good casting starts with your feet (or the boat), so to the extent you can slip into position to make a perfect (shorter) cast, that's great. But know your limits, and understand that the carp you target has a very finite zone when it comes to tolerances. In the best case, you can slide stealthily into position and make a short, accurate cast. Many other times, you're left with only one option—cast your fly out there as far and accurately as you can, and pray for a good outcome.

Above, lift and stop and below, make the cast! *Photos by Michael Frasier*

HINT: THE REPEAT CAST

Unless you're Superman (or Superwoman), when it comes to feeding carp you're going to make casts that miss the mark, in any scenario. Yes, your odds do decrease dramatically with every repeat cast, but there are ways to minimize that effect.

For one, you want to avoid the impulse to immediately rip a bad cast out of the zone and cast again. It's always best to wait awhile, let the fly settle to the bottom, and then slowly and subtly retrieve your line and fly in a way that lets you reload for the second shot. Never, ever pull a fly aggressively out of the zone where a carp might see it, even if that's a few feet or yards away. It's better to let the cruiser swim by, and then pull the fly out of the zone when it's obviously out of its limited field of vision.

Sometimes, the bad cast is worth waiting for. If you lead the fish too far, let the fly sink to the bottom and simply wait. So long as the carp is swimming in the general direction of that fly, you're still in the game. Wait. Maybe strip your line lightly so the fly flutters into the carp's path, and then pause again. Hold on until you know the fish and the fly are in the same arena, then give the fly a little twitch or two. Sometimes, an errant cast that leads the fish too much can turn into the perfect presentation, so long as you have the patience and subtle moves to work the fly into the feeding lane.

PRESENTATION

How you present a fly to carp is the number one factor that dictates whether the fish will eat it or not.

One of the tricks when fishing for carp is deciding exactly what they are eating, and because carp are perhaps the supreme piscine omnivores (they eat almost anything) this makes matters tough. So for now, let's focus on a few simple things.

First of all, understand that carp chase food with all their senses, from smell to vision. That's bad news for the purist fly angler. Conventional fishing for carp fishing revolves heavily around things like scents, "glugs," syrups, and things that make baits as stinky and attractive (at least to carp) as possible.

In my humble opinion, scents have no place in fly fishing of any sort. You can stink up your flies if you want to, soak them in buckets of chicken livers, spray the goop on them, and all that. But the moment you do so, you aren't fly fishing anymore. You're fishing a bait that once was a fly.

Fly anglers embrace challenges—or else, let's face it, we wouldn't be fly anglers in the first place). In the carp context, that main challenge is prompting a visually driven reaction in what is normally a scent-driven world.

So the deal is this: It doesn't matter if you're in a lake or a river, in clear water or dirty water, cold water or warm water, and so on. You must land your fly in a zone within inches (not feet) of where the carp is feeding.

The perfect carp cast drops a fly between 8 and 12 inches directly in front of the fish, as quickly and quietly as possible, without causing the fish to spook.

Much farther than that, and the carp won't see it. Hit the carp in the head and (of course) it won't eat the fly.

Think of it like this. Imagine the carp is wearing a baseball cap. (Sounds silly, I know, but stick with me here, and you'll understand my logic.) You want that fly to land almost exactly in line with the brim of that imaginary baseball cap. Inside that brim, you're too close, and will probably spook the fish. Outside that brim, and you're too far, and the carp may or may not see it. Of course you can wait and hope for the carp to swim to your fly. When I'm 6 inches too far away, I always opt to let the fly sit, and hope the carp will swim into range, rather than risk ripping the fly away and making another cast. The commotion of a recast is

Photo by Al Quattrocchi

Photo by Erin Block

usually a deal breaker. Best to ride it out and hope for the best when you're close but not perfectly on the money.

As when wearing a baseball cap, the field of vision is primarily pointing forward. Too far on the periphery is no good. Stick it on the bill of the cap, and you're halfway there.

Now you have to make the fly behave.

In trout fishing, it's important to put the dry fly on or in the water, and let it drift to the trout naturally. But carp fishing is like most saltwater situations, where the angler's imperative is to put the fly in plain sight, but then make it act as if it were trying to escape.

The best lesson I ever learned in that regard happened on Biscayne Bay in Florida, as I was fishing with the great flats legend Bill Curtis. Bill was on the platform, and I was on the bow of his skiff Grasshopper, when we both saw a big permit cruise into view. It looked like an aluminum trash can lid shining under the surface. I made what I thought was the perfect cast, tossing a crab pattern 60 feet on a straight line and dropping it a few feet in front of, and a few feet just past, the cruising permit.

As the fish neared my fly, I gently skipped it along the bottom into what I thought would be the perfect strike zone. But when the permit took notice of the fly, it abruptly wheeled around and swam away.

Curtis had already climbed down from his poling platform, grumbling all the way.

"What happened?" I asked. "What did I do wrong? I thought I made the perfect cast!"

Bill deadpanned: "Permit aren't used to their bait attacking them."

Lesson learned.

And that lesson also applies to carp, perhaps more so than to any other freshwater fish.

You have to make the presentation mimic what's really going on. If carp are eating berries, grasshoppers, or other flotsam on the top, drift the fly naturally into their mouths.

I recently fished for carp on Lake Henshaw in southern California during grasshopper season in late June. The lake was still until the cattle in nearby fields started to move, and the wind picked up. As a result, grasshoppers were kicking out of the fields and riding that breeze as long as they could, often plopping down helplessly into the ripples on the lake.

And, by quirky instinct, the carp were there waiting for them—often podded up in feeding clumps, their collective lips forming odd circles on the surface. Drop a fly into that mix, which wasn't easy given the whipping breeze, and it was a surefire take.

If, on the other hand, carp are grubbing along the bottom, perhaps kicking up clouds of silt that reveal their presence, you want to drop your fly on the edge of the silt and let it sink. A twitch here and there will often be enough to earn the bite.

When twitching flies along the bottom, you want to mix your cadence when it comes to the strip. Sometimes the long, slow pull works best with, for example, a crayfish pattern. Sometimes a short, choppy retrieve yields the hit. Mix your cadence, but when you find what's working, stick with it. Understand that this can change from day to day, even hour to hour, but mix and match your retrieve to find the bite, and stick with what the fish tell you to do.

When you see that single carp cruising along the bottom on a river flat or at the edge of a lake, hit him in the head. Well, not literally. But put that fly closer than your trout or bonefish instincts tell you to do.

Drop it right in the zone. And then make it move, as quickly as possible. That movement, however, should sometimes be no more than a scant twitch. But more often than not, it must move for the carp to want to eat it.

HINT: FIND YOUR CADENCE

When you're stripping carp flies, the "cadence" (how much line you pull per strip, and how quickly you do so) matters. Sometimes, in some places, you'll do best with long, slow strips, while at other times you'll do better with short, abrupt strips. Of course, a lot of that has to do with the fly you are using and what you are trying to imitate. But you are smart to mix it up until you find what works, and then stick with that. If 2-inch strips every 2 seconds yields a bite, stay with it. The cadence can vary from day to day, even in the same place, and using the same flies, so every day should be a new experiment.

Photo at right by Kevin Morlock

PART THREE · SCENARIOS

Photo by Tim Romano

Fighting Carp

20

A carp can eat a fly in many ways. Sometimes you'll feel a sudden "thunk" that sends a shock up your arm that's so intense, you'll fell as if you've hooked a freight train. At other times, you'll barely feel a thing; it's almost exactly like a trout inhaling a tiny nymph fly. I know anglers who will resort to drifting nymph flies under strike indicators for carp, exactly as they would on certain trout streams. To me, that seems to defeat the purpose. If you want to go play "bobber ball" for trout, go for it. But if you want to chase carp with flies, let's lose the training wheels.

When you're dancing flies along the bottom of a river or a lake, you want to do so with slow, deliberate, and subtle strips of the fly line. When you feel even the slightest resistance, strip-set the hook: Pull the fly line sharply with your off hand to drive the point of that hook into the carp's mouth. If you feel a thunk and strip-set, but don't come tight, keep stripping. Oftentimes a committed carp will continue the chase until it inhales that fly. If nothing happens, so what? You tried. Feeling the bite but then stopping your fly dead in the water to wait for something to happen is a surefire way to prevent a carp from eating your bug.

Carp fishing is frequently about seeing the actual eat. You won't feel it, but if a carp tips its head at a nymph suspended in the water column, perhaps flares its gills, or even if the fly disappears out of sight, for goodness sake, set the hook. The hook-set doesn't have to be much more than a strip of the line, or lifting your rod only as much as it would take to answer a telephone, pulling the handset to your ear. As when fishing for bonefish and other saltwater species, I much prefer the strip-set to trying to set the hook on a carp by lifting the rod tip, as I do when trout fishing. But you can get it done either way.

When the fish is firmly buttoned on, you want to let it run. Don't grab the reel, or try to apply the brakes. Strip in any slack in the line by hand if the carp runs toward you—but if it runs away, all you want to do is maintain constant pressure. The arc of your rod will tell you if you're doing it right or not. You want a steady "C" shape. When that becomes an upside-down "U," you know you're applying too much pressure, and even if you're using heavy leader and tippet materials, there's a good chance you're going to break the line—if you're lucky enough not to break your rod). If the rod stands straight up, and looks like an "I," you're not applying enough pressure, and the carp may well spit the fly.

From there, don't be afraid to tilt your rod to the side, and steer that fish, almost as if you were using the reins to steer a horse with a bit in its mouth. The more you keep the fish moving, the more tired it gets, and the sooner the fight ends, hopefully in your favor. Know the tolerances of your tackle, fly line, and tippet, but use that disk-drag reel to its full advantage. Get your money's worth. Make the fish fight the line, then the reel, then the rod, in that order. By keeping the rod flexed low—you don't want to play maypole games with carp as you would with trout—you'll improve your chances of landing the fish exponentially.

Steering a fish with the rod

Photo by Cameron Mortenson

Justin Watkins drags a carp to net.
Photo courtesy of John Bartlett

Better yet, if you actually stick your rod tip into the water as you try to steer the carp left or right, you'll gain more leverage. Steering a fish from above (with the tip in the air) is far less effective than "pulling" a carp under the surface, especially when you are working with heavy leader and tippet.

When the "endgame" approaches (and you'll know this because the carp's head will breach the surface) keep the pressure on and finish. When the fish points toward the bottom, the fight is still on. But once its nose pops above the surface, you have all the leverage, and the fish has, for all intents and purposes, quit. Lift the rod tip high, and drag the fish to the net.

Game over.

Photo by Kevin Morlock

Freeing Carp

21

*F*or the catch-and-release angler, the game isn't quite over. After you land the fish is when you transition from hunter to healer.

If you want to release the carp, handle it with wet hands, keep your fingers away from its gills, remove the fly as gingerly and gently as possible, hold it upright in the water until it regains its strength, and then let it swim away. The perfect catch-and-release actually requires little if any contact with the fish at all. Net it, reach down and pop the fly loose, allow the fish to regain its bearings, and then let it swim out of the net. No slime is no crime, and the less your hands smell like carp at day's end, the more you—and the fish—can be considered winners.

HINT: HOLD YOUR BREATH

If you wonder how long it's okay to hold a carp out of the water as you take photos and so forth, just hold your breath as you snap the pictures. When you get uncomfortable, it's safe to assume the carp is also feeling that way. Even though carp are among the toughest fish in the world, the one thing that will kill them quickest is oxygen deprivation, and they need to be in the water to breathe.

Preparing to release a Lake Michigan carp
Photo by Tim Romano

Photo by Tim Romano

Berry Fishing

22

*O*ne of the most exotic fishing experiences I've ever had was chasing pacu on jungle rivers in Bolivia. Pacu are large, oblong, permit-shaped fish, and they thrive on plants and berries that fall into the water. They're notoriously spooky, but if you can sneak up on one and make the right cast, there's just something peculiar and captivating about watching a fish like that eat flora off the surface. So I traveled to the upper headwaters of the Amazon and camped among the rivers, where jaguars prowl and anacondas swim, in order to experience that.

And then I came home to the United States and, several months later, went mulberry fishing for carp in an urban riverscape, and experienced basically the same phenomenon. Granted, there weren't monkeys howling in the trees and macaws flying overhead, and the shadows cast on the river's surface weren't caused by a jungle canopy, but rather tall concrete buildings, but within that tightly focused space where the fishing action occurred, it was remarkably similar. Again, the beauty of carp fishing is that it often involves the exotic and unexpected, right outside the back door.

The trick when berry fishing is using flies that not only imitate the shapes and colors of the berries that fall into the water, but also—perhaps more importantly—mimic their weight and buoyancy. Keith Curley is a master of the mulberry, and though he made me take a vow of secrecy so I wouldn't reveal his favorite Mid-Atlantic region carp spot, he shared a technique that applies to almost any spot where berries drop in water where carp swim.

Earlier in the season, white and lighter shades work best, while darker colors are optimal when the berries mature. A fly that drops like a bead and sinks like a rock is no good. Same for a fly that lands in the water but floats like a bug. You want a fly that will land with an authentic "plop" and then sink slowly and deliberately into the feeding zone, and it's best if they remain suspended in the current

Photo by Tim Romano

Mulberries and flies tied to imitate them. *Photo by Cameron Mortenson*

for a long time. For that reason, fuzzy textures and soft materials work best, and flashy accents like Mylar are also bonuses.

Chris Hunt, who wrote the foreword to this book, related an experience where he watched carp turn on his berry fly after it landed in the water, only to swim within inches, its eyeball closely inspecting the fly as it drifted downstream, before finally eating it. It's that level of scrutiny that makes the berry fishing game so tricky, and ultimately appealing for the carp angler.

I believe my odds of hooking carp with berry flies are at least ten times better when I'm making a downstream presentation, rather than casting upstream. Make the cast, throw in a big upstream mend, and let the fly do its thing. It's important to have the fly itself be the first thing that floats into the zone, rather than fly line, tippet, and so forth. I also almost never cast berries while I'm standing in the water. It's best to stand on the bank, mindful of your shadow, of course.

Photo by Tim Romano

How and Why I Blew It at the South Platte River Pro-Am Carp Slam

23

*W*henever I fish anywhere, for any species, I make it a habit at day's end, perhaps as I'm nodding off to sleep at night, to go through the "game film." There is seldom any real film, of course, but I think it helps me as an angler to recount certain scenarios in my mind, and think through what I might have done differently, what I did perfectly, and most importantly, what I'd do next time, given the same circumstances and opportunities.

I recently fished the Sixth Annual South Platte River Pro-Am Carp Slam, and didn't land a single carp. That's not necessarily a cause for shame—with 30 anglers competing, only 14 fish were landed, and some of the anglers caught multiple carp, so there were plenty of "zero-fers" to go around. But I actually hooked two fish (three fish won the tournament) and didn't land either. One broke off, and the other spit the fly. I could have been in the money.

The tournament was divided into a morning and an afternoon session. The morning was cloudy, and the water on the beat we drew was dark and murky. We didn't see a single fish. Luck of the draw. I can accept that.

Incidentally, nobody in the tournament caught a single fish; had I made something happen then, I would have earned hero status. But in the afternoon, we had clear water, and immediately I was able to spot fish as I walked the riverbank. There were a few in a glide below a riffle. We stopped and made a few casts, but pressed on upstream, where we found dozens of carp swimming like trout in a dark run. That's where I hooked (and lost) my fish. But I had goofed up much sooner than that.

You see, in hindsight, I realize that those fish in the "trout run" were cruising about, but they weren't feeding with any deliberation. The fish in the glide below, on the other hand, were definite players, tilting and weaving in the current as they fed.

Mistake number one is that I left a few feeding fish to go find more nonfeeding fish. Never leave a feeding carp to chase other opportunities. Fish to that target until it either eats, or you know it's definitely on to you.

Carp in what looks like a trout run.
Photo by Brian Bradfield

Mistake number two was that, when I saw all those carp collected in one place, I didn't take the time to watch them, and separate the legitimate targets from the decoys, before I started blindly casting. Were I on my own, and not in a competition and on the clock, I would have sat down on the bank and observed. But I went headlong right into the mix, and tried to enforce my will on the fish. Two fish were dumb enough to fall for it. But I lost them both.

And then, as I grew more frustrated, I started to march along the river and cast with more frequency, when I should have stopped, regrouped, and waited for the fish to come around. With every cast I made, it seemed that I saw fewer and fewer targets. I ultimately cast myself right out of contention.

It's always worth slowing down when carp fishing.

And whether you're in a tournament or not, the team approach—with one angler making the casts, and his or her partner calling in the shots and coaching, is always a good idea.

Next time, I'm going to be a more patient, pragmatic team player.

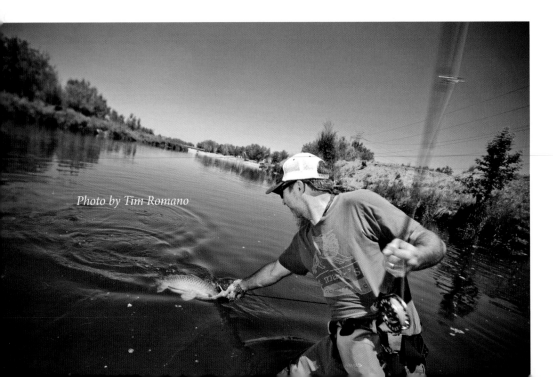

Photo by Tim Romano

From the Experts: Their Best Tips in Their Own Words

24

*Y*ou certainly shouldn't take everything I say as gospel when it comes to fly fishing for carp. I'm still learning as I go—as is anyone who honestly assesses their understanding of both fly fishing and carp fishing. But to round things off, and perhaps drive home some of the points I've made with more effect, I asked some of the most dedicated and successful carp-focused fly fishermen I know to share their own perspectives and insights, their "A-list" tips, and here's what they had to say:

Barry Reynolds, coauthor of *Carp on the Fly: A Fly Fishing Guide:*

"Do not 'sit' on a single fish too long. For practical purposes, it's a numbers game. You want to find the right fish in the right situation. Cover water. Look and learn. Find a player. If the fish don't react the way you want them to at first, leave them alone, remember where they are, and come back to them later. If you pester them too much, you'll ruin all opportunity. You cannot beat a carp into submission."

Bonus tip: The one thing Barry has learned in the past 15 years, since first publishing Carp on the Fly:

"I've gone smaller on the flies. I fish a size 12 soft-hackle more than you might imagine. Pressure has dictated that. The more people fly fish for carp on the South Platte, the more fickle the fish get. But there are still ways to trick carp. Sometimes, suspending a small nymph in front of a carp, and actually watching the fish eat the fly can be more challenging. But it's also more rewarding."*

*Reynolds, et al. *Carp on the Fly,* p. 13

Bruce Smithhammer, manager of High Country Flies
(highcountryflies.com), outdoor writer (*The Drake,
Angling Trade,* and elsewhere) and co-conspirator
of the "Buster Wants to Fish" (busterwantstofish.com) blog:

"If there was one single tip I could offer a carp beginner, it's the 'FFF' rule: Find feeding fish. It's nothing profound, but it's the one thing that I see a lot of carp noobs wasting their time on—fish that aren't actually feeding, particularly the jumpers. It's really tempting when you see carp leaping out of the water to fire a cast at them, but I have never once seen a jumping carp eat."

Jeff Currier, world traveler, artist, and author of *Currier's Quick
and Easy Guide to Warmwater Fly Fishing* (jeffcurrier.com):

"I travel around the world in search of new species, because those new species represent challenges. But carp are the species that are close to home, yet I know I'll never fully conquer them. When I fish for trout, I have a pretty good idea what my max catch will be, but carp will surprise you. And they're cool fish, with cartoon character faces. You look at those vibrant eyes, and they look back at you, as if to say, 'You won today, but I'll win tomorrow.' My tip would be to mix things up a lot. You can find a fly that works three times in a row, but then won't work for the next seven times straight. I like to throw saltwater flies, like Root Beer Crazy Charleys and Gotchas. Your presentation depends on what's happening on the bottom. If it's grassy, you might want to avoid the snag, but there are a thousand ways to present a single fly."

Michael Gracie of Trout's Fly Fishing in Denver, noted carp chaser,
and voice behind the blog michaelgracie.com:

"You have to hide in the bushes and wait. The more carp fishermen act like duck hunters, the better they are."

John Bartlett, mastermind of carponthefly.blogspot.com:

"When it comes to fishing for carp in water where it's not so easy to detect the take, intentionally try to cast your fly 2 or 3 inches to the left or right side of its head. When you see the fish turn, you'll know when to set the hook. I've made many perfect casts directly in front of the fish, only to miss the strike because I couldn't tell what the fish was doing. If you put it in a place where you know the fish will see it, but it has to move even slightly to pick up that fly, you'll know exactly when the eat happens."

Dave Maynard, outdoors television personality, guide, writer, and photographer:

"When you walk up to the river, be ready to cast. Do all your spotting and knot tying and all those things from a distance. But when you're ready to cast, step right up there, fly in hand. Don't mess around, don't talk, don't watch and wait. Fire the cast. I am convinced that carp can sense vibrations on the land. I've seen more carp spooked by people walking along the water (but not in it) than any other fish."

Ryan Dunne, Appalachian Fly Guides (appflyguides.wordpress.com):

"When it comes to fly materials, I haven't noticed a difference in carp behavior toward either natural or synthetic materials. However, most of my fly patterns contain a combination of both."

Clint Packo, owner of Freestone Aquatics, guide, and co-champion (with Will Rice) of the South Platte River Pro-Am Carp Slam:

"Watch fish behavior, and treat each fish individually. That might mean different casts, different flies, and so forth. Don't assume a template for many fish. Approach each fish as a unique and individual problem to solve."

Will Rice, writer (*Angling Trade, The Drake,* and elsewhere) and co-champion of the South Platte River Pro-Am Carp Slam:

"Understand that carp fishing is hard. Don't get discouraged. Keep after it. Know that once you think you have it figured out, it will all change again. That is part of the game, and it keeps you thinking and coming back to the water."

David Moore, Euro-style carp angling champion, tournament director, and owner of Big Carp Tackle (bigcarptackle.com):

"Don't be afraid to think outside the box. I think a lot of fly anglers lean on their trout-fishing instincts too much, using subtle colors on flies and so forth. Carp are curious critters. Bright colors work great. Another thing I've noticed is that fly guys move too fast. If you have the right rig, don't move it. Have patience, and let the fish work to you."

J.P. Lipton, mastermind of roughfisher.com:

"Understand that different types of water present different carp-fishing scenarios and opportunities. The carp in a river should not be expected to act and eat the exact same way as the carp in a lake. An angler should tune into the different complexities of each environment, and the better they understand both, the more adept they'll be at catching carp with flies everywhere."

Chris Hunt, national communications director of Trout Unlimited, voice behind the eatmorebrooktrout.com blog, and avid (closet) carp junkie:

"When you're fishing a fly on the carp flats, it all revolves around a slow retrieve of the fly. A subtle twitch . . . that painstakingly deliberate motion . . . and if you feel any resistance at all, you should strip-set the fly."

Kevin Morlock, Indigo Guide Service (indigoguideservice.com), Walhalla and Beaver Island, Michigan:

"I think a carp angler should understand that the fish they chase often assume characteristics akin to the waters in which they live. Pond carp are pond carp, but a Great Lakes carp has almost 'oceanic' tendencies, in that they wander far, they chase big baits, and they react on the movement of the water. Don't ever assume that carp fishing is a one-size-fits-all endeavor."

Geoff Mueller, senior editor of *The Drake* and winner of the Bighorn River Alliance Carp Festival, 2012:

"Feed the fish. Carp can be stubborn eaters and will ignore seemingly well-presented flies, over and over. More often than not, 'seemingly,' it seems, is not good enough. If you have a captive audience of carp that remains in an area, milling around, despite your presence and a multitude of shunned presentations, there's a good chance a player or two remains in the mix. We've spent patient minutes working specific pods, only to finally score a hook-up after a planet-aligning presentation. The lesson: Don't give up on carp until you're convinced they've given up on you. A carp's feeding window is relatively small, for instance, compared to a trout that may travel from Livingston to Billings to crush an articulated streamer. Instead, focus on a fly-meets-lips presentation to seal the deal."

Conway Bowman, author of *The Orvis Guide to Saltwater Fly Fishing* and host of *Fly Fishing the World* on The Sportsman Channel:

"Carp fishing is all about making an accurate cast. You can't use the haymaker cast to fish for carp and expect to be successful. You get one shot, so make it count. Also, it's important to read the fish according to the season. Spawning fish act differently than feeding fish on the flats. So understand that, and plan your flies and presentations accordingly."

Tim Romano, managing editor of *Angling Trade* magazine and co-editor of the fly-fishing blog "Fly Talk" at fieldandstream.com:

"I honestly and truly think that once you get to a 'fishy' spot you should conceal yourself as much as possible and sit and watch. Watch the fish. Watch the birds.

Watch what the cars do, and what the people on the bike path do. Watch what tree limbs are doing blowing in the wind. Then take all this info and see what the fish does in response to them all. Including yourself. Then after five or ten minutes, make a plan of attack and don't break it. Go with your gut and what you've just absorbed and try to catch the fish based on what will not spook it."

John Hendrickson, manager of the San Diego Fly Shop and winner of the 2012 Lake Henshaw (California) Warm Water Throwdown: (carpthrowdown.com):

"My tip is get a secret family doughball recipe that's been handed down through generations, and memorize it word for word! Can you use that? Ha Ha Ha. (That wouldn't be funny, but for the fact that a Hendrickson secret family doughball recipe actually exists.) In terms of fly fishing, my advice would translate to 'being as observant as humanly possible.' Fly fishing for carp requires you not only to fish, but also to hunt. And a hunter cannot be successful without being observant."

Steve Martinez, Indigo Guide Service, Walhalla and Beaver Island, Michigan:

"How you move a fly is as important as what the fly actually looks like in the first place. It has to act real. Looking real isn't nearly enough . . . at least not for carp."

Jay Zimmerman, guide and professional fly tier:

"Get your fly in front of as many carp as possible. Stalk the dikes, banks, and mud flats with line off the reel, fly in hand, ready to get a shot off at a moment's notice. Your window of opportunity is often very small. You usually will only have a one-cast opportunity, so have a rod and line you are comfortable with (even if it is too light to be considered a proper 'carp rod'). And always know where your fly is, be in control of it once it is in the water . . . I can't stress the importance of this enough."

Erin Block, contract fly designer, author, and blogger at mysteriesinternal.blogspot.com:

"It's a brain game, really. And short-term memory is one of the most important things you can have when fly fishing for carp. You'll feel like a failure most of the time, and you'll be right. But you have to be able to forget what you've done wrong, the ones you've spooked, opportunities you've missed: You have to be able to move forward and keep on casting. Fly fishing for carp requires mental fortitude as much as it does skill."

Captain Paul Rose of Carolina Bonefishing
(carolinabonefishing.com):

"I can quickly teach clients where to look, spotting fish, stealth, approach, and presentation, all of which are important. But the problem is putting all this info together quickly and then detecting the strike. Because it is a very visual game versus the more common tactile feel (a tug on the line), most anglers miss the take. Anglers must learn to read a carp's body language and attitude. A flared gill, darting forward, tail tipping, and lip protrusion all are indicative of a take. If you wait to feel a strike, you are too late. Carp spit offerings fast. Many anglers stand on the bow with rod in one arm, head down, shoulders shrugged as they look back at me and ask, 'Did he just eat?' I often prompt anglers with 'Now!' the first few times a fish eats. Once they get the strip strike, the success rate goes up."

Tim Daughton, product development specialist for
The Orvis Company and self-professed "carpaholic":

"My absolute number one tip is to slow down. Spend time watching the fish. See how they feed, where they feed, and when. Go slow when getting into position to present your fly to a feeding fish. Don't rush, because you may get only one or two shots at a fish. Don't be in a hurry to cast, which is easier said than done when you have a fish feeding right in from of you. Get into position, watch the fish, determine the best presentation, and then, and only then, make your cast. I spend more time scouting, spotting, and stalking than I do casting. I have learned so much just watching them, and I firmly believe it has greatly improved my success, although I routinely get schooled by these finicky fish."

Photo by Steve Martinez

Grass carp (*Ctenopharyngodon idella*)
Photo by Mabon Childs

Grass Carp

25

When you think you have a good handle on catching common carp with flies, and you need another healthy dose of humility, go ahead and try to figure out how to catch grass carp with flies. I'll be perfectly honest with you. I can count on my fingers the number of grass carp I have caught with flies. That's partly because grass carp are about 100 times harder to trick into eating a fly, and partly because I realize that well enough to avoid bruising my ego by dedicating a lot of time and effort to grass carp.

Nonetheless, grass carp are amazing creatures—some would argue they are the ultimate carp. They are vegetarians, but they grow to immense sizes. They don't have the sagging bellies of common carp and mirror carp. You can tell the difference between common carp and grass carp when you see them in a pond, partly because grass carp tend to have darker backs and more silvery profiles, but mostly because they are more streamlined, even torpedo shaped. The mouth of a grass carp is typically more forward than the vacuuming, downward-pointing sucker mouth of the common carp. And grass carp are better fighters, no doubt. They pull harder, swerve and veer, and even jump from time to time.

If you hook and land a grass carp of any size, you should be proud, because that is indeed one of the top challenges in the entire world of fly angling.

So how do you do it?

Most of the carp anglers I know who have caught many grass carp will say the same thing: The conditions have to be right. It's almost like the sun, moon, and stars line up just so, the wind blows, and grass carp dramatically change from being ultraselective to gluttons. When you get a steady wind blowing plant matter into a pond or lake, that's the time to start thinking about catching grass carp.

Because grass carp eat vegetation, your fly should look very natural—green, brown, and yellow flies are key. The best fly I've ever seen for grass carp is the Puff pattern developed by Kent Klewein, who along with Louis Cahill runs the "Gink and Gasoline" (ginkandgasoline.com) blog. It's a spongy, green fly that lands softly, and most importantly suspends in the water column after it lands.

FIND OUT MORE ABOUT "GINK AND GASOLINE"

That brings up another important distinction between grass carp and common carp. With common carp, your best "players" are feeding on the bottom. Your next best options are the ones you find feeding on the surface. And the common carp you are least likely to hook is the one suspended in the middle. With grass carp, if you can see them feeding on the surface, you have a decent chance. The suspended fish is also an opportunity. But it's really, really hard to hook a grass carp when it's lying on the bottom.

Another important difference between fishing for common carp and grass carp is that, because grass carp eat inanimate plant matter, it's paramount to let a fly drift as naturally as possible. No twitches, no jerks. (Okay, you might make an errant cast and feel the need to drag the fly into the feeding zone, but by and large that won't work.) You need to hit them in the head, and hope for the best.

As far as tackle is concerned, I use the same rod, reel, line, and so forth, but I am a very big believer in using lighter-weight fluorocarbon tippets when it comes to fishing for grass carp.

The last challenge with grass carp is detecting the "eat." They exclusively inhale food, meaning you'll almost never feel a pronounced thunk, and since you're almost always fishing flies that are drifting in the current (rather than stripping or twitching significantly) you need to depend on your eyes to tell you when to set the hook.

When in doubt, set the hook. Use a strip-set. In the worst case, you move the fly in a way that spooks the fish. This is grass carp fishing, after all. You're going to spook fish no matter what you do, and if you come up connected, you're a hero.

HINT: GREASE YOUR LEADER

Because so many grass carp strikes are difficult to detect, I like to add a dab of fly floatant to my leader or tippet, a foot or so above my fly, depending on the depth I'm trying to fish and the speed of the surface current. That greased section of leader or tippet creates a dimple where the line descends below the surface, and that can work as a de facto strike indicator. It's no different from using a strike indicator for trout fishing. At the first sign of the slightest disturbance, go ahead and set the hook.

Carp Trivia

26

*Photo by
Tim Romano*

$\mathcal{M}$ost people find the carp among the ugliest of fish, and the goldfish and the koi the prettiest. These are exactly the same species, *Cyprinus carpio*. Various color varieties were developed using selective breeding in Japan and China long ago, while Europe was busy with feudalism. The most beautiful and expensive show fish in the world are now called koi.

In 1879, the German common carp was brought from the reflecting pool of the Washington Monument in a railroad "fish" car by the U.S. Commission on Fish and Fisheries and dumped from the railroad bridge just below the confluence of Cherry Creek and the South Platte River in Denver. The purpose was to provide fresh fish to Denver because the South Platte had been overfished and polluted. Like many grand plans, the food fish idea didn't last long in Denver, or anywhere else in America. We have all been raised to despise the carp as ugly and a nuisance.

There were already "native carp" (the Colorado pikeminnow or squawfish) in Colorado's South Platte River when the German (common) carp were introduced.

The common carp is more highly evolved than the trout. The carp has better hearing, a better sense of smell, eats a wider range of foods, and can actually breathe oxygen by gulping air on the surface.

The eggs and fry produced by carp are now an important food source for herons, otters, and largemouth bass.

Millions of pounds of Mississippi River carp become gefilte fish each year.

Large koi caught on a fly. *Photo by Adam Hope.*

When a fish, a fruit, or a fashion falls out of favor, the only solution to social acceptance is a name change. War bonnets have come back, to every fly tier's disgust, as feather hair extensions. The Chinese gooseberry, as everyone knows, was renamed the kiwi. The slimefish was renamed orange roughy, and the Patagonia toothfish was renamed the Chilean sea bass. Grass carp were recently renamed white amur. But the much-maligned common carp in the South Platte is still the carp after 130 years. Maybe "Colorado dorado" would work.

(Courtesy of John H. Davenport, author of Freedom for the River Queen*)*

Photo by Chris Hunt

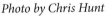

Afterword

I know that I can talk about fly fishing for carp until my face turns blue. I hope you realize that all I've written thus far is based on lessons I've learned—some through trial and error, and others by listening to and experiencing what others had to show me. Being an "enlightened" fly fisherman, or fly-fishing writer, is really all about coming to the understanding that it's impossible for anyone to fully understand any of this alone, especially when it comes to carp. The more you learn, the more you realize how much is yet to be understood.

I've tried to give you some useful advice that may, hopefully, shorten your learning curve and turn you onto fishing for carp with a fly rod. Because I honestly think that the more people dabble with carp on the fly, the more anglers we'll recruit into a fold that protects all gamefish, in salt water and fresh. All are important to me. I also think that by spreading the load onto carp, we might ease some pressure on trout. Most importantly, I think that if you want to be a great fly angler, and not just a dabbler, carp will eventually fit into your plans.

I've traveled all over the world and have caught many fish, but nothing brings out the best of me the way carp can. I really mean that. But this is still a new frontier, and I'm admittedly still learning. Hopefully you will, too.

PHILANTHROPY

We at Stonefly Press feel that it's important to view ourselves as a small part of a greater system of balance. We give back to that which nourishes us because it feels natural and right.

Stonefly Press will be donating a portion of our annual profits to conservation groups active in environmental stewardship. We encourage all our readers to learn more about them here, and encourage you to go a step further and get involved.

American Rivers
(americanrivers.org)

Friends of the White River
(friendsofwhiteriver.org)

Bonefish & Tarpon Trust
(bonefishtarpontrust.org)

Riverkeeper
(riverkeeper.org)

California Trout
(caltrout.org)

Trout Unlimited
(tu.org)

Coastal Conservation Association
(joincca.org)

Western Rivers Conservancy
(westernrivers.org)

INDEX

Note: Page numbers in **bold** indicate illustrations.

A

Access to fly fishing, 15
All-Purpose Nymph fly, **103**
Anal fin, **29**
Asian carp, 21, **21**
Attractor fly, 52

B

Backstabber fly, **96**
Baitfish, 48, 50
Barbels, 28, **29**
Bartlett, John, 44, 128
BC Hopper-Dropper fly, **98**
Beadhead Soft-hackle Pheasant
    Tail fly, **101**
Beaver Island, 30
Befus, Brad, 13
Benson (female carp), 27
Berry fishing, 121–123
Berry flies, **122**
Berryman, John, 13
Biscayne Bay, 110
Block, Erin, **xiii**, **40**, 131
Boots, 70–71, **71**
Bowman, Conway, **50**, 86, 130
Breathable waders, **71**
Breer, Denny, 34
Brown trout, 19–21, **19**, **20**

C

Cadence, 111
Cahill, Louis, 135

Carp
abundance of, 15
environmental requirements,
    23–25, 33–35, **34**, **35**
feeding differences by habitat,
    41–44
feeding methods, 51–52, 89–93
as food, 137–138
food sources, 47–50, **49**
gulping air, **25**
introduction into Denver, 137
as invasive species, 23
lifespan, 25
physical characteristics of,
    27–31
releasing, **120**
senses of, 27–31
social behavior, 37–39, **38**
See also Asian carp; common
    carp; grass carp; mirror carp
Carp Bitters fly, **103**
Carp fly fishing
approach, 75–77
berry fishing, 121–123
casting, 105–108
catch-and-release, 119
choosing flies, 95–96
difficulty of, 57–58
by feeding method, 89–93
fighting carp, 115–117
finding fish, 79–87
lessons learned, 125–126

patterns, 11–13
presentation, 108–111
prioritizing carp, 93
reasons for, 7–8
tips from experts, 127–132
*Carp on the Fly: A Fly-fishing
    Guide*, 13
Casting
effect of lines on, 68
method for, 105–108
presentation, 108–111
for river carp, 77
Catch-and-release, 119
Caudal fin, **29**
Choosing flies, 95–96
Chumming, 30
Clinch knot, 70
Clouser Minnow fly, **99**
Color of lines, 68
Columbia River, 44
Common carp, **19**, **21**
biology of, 23–25
grass carp versus, 135–136
introduction into America,
    19–21
in South Platte River, 137
The Compleat Angler (Walton),
    ix
Copper John fly, **100**
Costas polarized sunglasses, **82**
Crayfish, 47
Crazy Charley fly, **102**